ASCD MEMBER BOOK

Many ASCD members received this book as a
member benefit upon its initial release.

Learn more at: **www.ascd.org/memberbooks**

AARON TAIT + DAVE FAULKNER

DREAM
TEAM

A Practical Playbook to
Help **Innovative Educators**
Change Schools

ASCD
Alexandria, Virginia USA

1703 N. Beauregard St. • Alexandria, VA 22311-1714 USA
Phone: 800-933-2723 or 703-578-9600 • Fax: 703-575-5400
Website: www.ascd.org • E-mail: member@ascd.org
Author guidelines: www.ascd.org/write

Deborah S. Delisle, *Executive Director;* Stefani Roth, *Publisher;* Genny Ostertag, *Director, Content Acquisition;* Susan Hills, *Acquisitions Editor;* Julie Houtz, *Director, Book Editing & Production;* Katie Martin, *Editor;* Judi Connelly, *Associate Art Director;* Thomas Lytle, *Senior Graphic Designer;* Cynthia Stock, *Typesetter;* Mike Kalyan, Director, *Production Services;* Trinay Blake, *E-Publishing Specialist*

All web links in this book are correct as of the publication date below but may have become inactive or otherwise modified since that time. If you notice a deactivated or changed link, please e-mail books@ascd.org with the words "Link Update" in the subject line. In your message, please specify the web link, the book title, and the page number on which the link appears.

PAPERBACK ISBN: 978-1-4166-2661-9 ASCD product #119022
PDF E-BOOK ISBN: 978-1-4166-2663-3; see Books in Print for other formats.
Quantity discounts are available: e-mail programteam@ascd.org or call 800-933-2723, ext. 5773, or 703-575-5773. For desk copies, go to www.ascd.org/deskcopy.

ASCD Member Book No. FY19-3 (Dec. 2018 P). ASCD Member Books mail to Premium (P), Select (S), and Institutional Plus (I+) members on this schedule: Jan, PSI+; Feb, P; Apr, PSI+; May, P; Jul, PSI+; Aug, P; Sep, PSI+; Nov, PSI+; Dec, P. For current details on membership, see www.ascd.org/membership.

Library of Congress Cataloging-in-Publication Data
Names: Tait, Aaron, author. | Faulkner, Dave, author.
Title: Dream team : a practical playbook to help innovative educators change schools / Aaron Tait and Dave Faulkner.
Description: Alexandria, Virginia. : ASCD, [2019] | Includes bibliographical references and index.
Identifiers: LCCN 2018037531 (print) | LCCN 2018039161 (ebook) | ISBN 9781416626633 (PDF) | ISBN 9781416626619 (pbk.)
Subjects: LCSH: School improvement programs. | Educational innovations. | Educational leadership. | Educational change. | School support teams.
Classification: LCC LB2822.8 (ebook) | LCC LB2822.8 .T35 2019 (print) | DDC 371.2/07—dc23
LC record available at https://lccn.loc.gov/2018037531

28 27 26 25 24 23 22 21 20 19   1 2 3 4 5 6 7 8 9 10 11 12

for our kids

DREAM TEAM

INTRODUCTION

The Challenge, the Way, and the Why
Dave Faulkner
Halls Creek, Western Australia, 2008

It was a new day for me, the principal of Halls Creek District School.

Some days would start with the piercing shriek of the alarm clock, but usually I was awake long before it rang, my mind already buzzing with a thousand things that had to get done, many of them roll-overs from old to-do lists. Other mornings, the bad dreams would wake me. Many principals have bad dreams. But today, it was the bird—a crow, to be exact, the one with a call that sounded a lot like a sick goat being hurled off a cliff and who liked to set up shop in a tree right next to our bedroom window. I opened one eye, reached for my phone, and glanced at the screen. It was Monday morning, barely light out, and I already had 33 e-mails, 7 texts, and 2 missed calls.

I rolled out of bed, and my running shoes were the first thing that I saw. They were filthy, covered in trash juice, which is a close contender for the worst-smelling thing on the planet. The local municipality had gone on strike last week, and with our school janitorial staff out sick, I had spent part of my Sunday hauling 50 large trash cans to the dump on the other side of town. It had topped 100 degrees every day for the past fortnight, so by the weekend, the bins were nasty—but not too nasty to keep my deputy from meeting me in the carpark at 8:00 a.m. without me even asking. A hero. After the final bin drop, I thanked him in his love language: a Snickers bar and a can of Red Bull.

Sundays were supposed to be my "revolutionary days," a chance to get some quiet time to work up new creative curricula or professional development activities for the staff. But between the trash bins, an unfriendly e-mail inbox, and a pile of administrative work I had to get through, this recent Sunday had been a 14-hour slog of reacting, not revolutionizing.

But today was a new day and a new school week, in one of the most remote towns in the world. We were in the Australian outback, red dirt country, 750 miles away from Darwin, the nearest main city. Most of the 1,000 people who lived in Halls Creek were Indigenous, and as small as the town was, it was well known as a center for culture and art. But Halls Creek also had its fair share of problems. An award-winning journalist wrote a major article describing it as "worse than a war zone" due to its levels of poverty, alcohol abuse, and violence. My family was from up this way; both my grandparents and parents had worked for years as missionaries in this part of the country, and my father had been a teacher here. Despite the many challenges Halls Creek faced, I loved it—and I loved the people who called it home.

I dressed quickly, grabbed a Red Bull from the fridge, and with a wide yawn, scooped up the keys to the school bus. Yes, it occasionally fell to me to drive the bus, and I actually kind of liked it. It was a great way to connect with the kids, and blasting some 90s-era INXS over the bus speakers usually did the trick to kick me into gear and ready me for another day as the principal of Halls Creek. But this week, the novelty was likely to wear off. With our regular guy away, I was on driving duty every morning.

As I turned the corner for the first pickup, I slowed the bus to a crawl to negotiate the scatterings of broken beer bottles that littered the road. There had clearly been some parties the night before—and I knew these parties meant many of my students who lived here wouldn't have been able to fall asleep until the early hours of the morning.

I pulled up to the first house and leaned on the horn, turning down the stereo to listen for signs of life. Other than the goat-killing noise of the crow, which was apparently following me, there was silence. Nothing newsworthy there—the Campbell kids were always slow to rise.

I put the bus in park, jogged up to the front door, and yelled out a cheery "Hey hey hey! Time for school!" I knocked heavily on the thin timber door, mindful not to pick up any splinters from the extra holes that had appeared over the weekend. "Shut the f--k up!" was the cheery greeting I received from the next-door neighbors. Also par for the course at the Campbell house. After a few seconds of waiting, I heard the pitter-patter of bare feet making their way toward me. My first win of the day.

One of my students opened the door, her head not quite through the neck of a stained sweater, a mop of unbrushed hair bleached blonde by the sun bursting out the top. Laughing, I pulled the sweater down and greeted my now-identified grade 6 student with a "Morning, Jess!" She responded with a shy smile and an open-mouthed yawn before stumbling toward the bus, her little brother trailing behind her.

The bus's first run was smaller than usual; I was right about the parties taking a toll. But with 13 kids (by now wide awake) on board, and INXS swapped out for a fun new rap tune from the kids' favorite band, we arrived at the school carpark in style. The kids were all out the door before I had fully opened it, bolting toward the breakfast station. I strolled over as well, tempted by the wafting aroma of bacon-and-egg sandwiches.

"Small run?" asked Alice, a teacher, offering me a roll wrapped in greasy wax paper.

"Afraid so," I responded. "Looks like the party was a big one last night."

I declined Alice's offer of breakfast—had to make sure all the kids were fed first—but she explained, "We have extra from the festival last week, so there is plenty to go around. And you are going to need it this week!" She didn't have to ask me again.

The second bus run took a little longer, the route a bit farther away. For some of the families out here, education was not the highest priority. I passed my own house on this run, and I grinned widely as I picked up my 5-year-old daughter, Grace, and Maddy, her best mate and the granddaughter of Auntie Lynn, a local elder who had been helping me out ever since I had taken the job the year before.

By 7:45, I was in the building and had a few moments for e-mails. I sat down at my desk and took a quick look down the hallway in front of me. Turning the desk to face outward was one of the first things I did when I moved into that new office—a clear symbol to my team that I was never too busy to chat with them. There had been quite a few offices for me over the last five years, the education minister having made it a habit to overestimate my ability to quickly turn around some of the tougher schools in the state.

The first two e-mails weren't great.

One was from a pair of teachers who had been away for the weekend. On their way home last night, their car had broken down 200 miles from Halls Creek; the repairs were going to take the whole day. The second e-mail was from a teacher who was taking a sick day and wanting to schedule a meeting with the visiting department psychologist. I didn't blame her. As a community, everyone was dealing with far more trauma and pain than a little town of this size would usually have to endure. A few suicides in our small community earlier in the year were now dangerously close to becoming a really scary trend.

So that was three teachers absent on this Monday. There were no relief teachers in Halls Creek, so my only option was to cancel the scheduled numeracy and literacy staff development sessions; all of us would be needed in classrooms. I sent the bad news via text message to Kate, a senior teacher, who had probably spent the better part of the weekend preparing for her one-on-ones with staff. Her response was quick and to the point: "SERIOUSLY?" I pressed the call button as soon as I saw it, kicking myself as I waited for Kate to pick up. I should have told her in person, not through a text. She was a brilliant teacher who really cared, and here I was, letting her down.

Classes started at 8:00, the schedule designed to squeeze in as much learning as possible before the heat of the day set in. I put myself in with grade 7, but just after 9:00, one of our newest teachers burst into my class saying she needed help. She was from the city and young, so my initial thought was that there probably wasn't much happening. Still, I caught the eye of Rose, my ever-capable assistant teacher, and she gave me a nod that said, *I've got it. Go.*

Turned out my initial thought was wrong. My walk across the courtyard soon turned into a jog and then into a sprint to break up two high school girls fighting on the pavement. Then there were egos and small wounds to be patched up in the sick bay and a traumatized teacher to calm. *Well, the visiting psychologist will soon have another patient or two,* I thought.

Just as things seemed to be getting under control, another fight broke out, and once again I found myself playing the role of a boxing umpire trying to get between two fighters. This time, though, the fighters weren't kids but *parents.* Yes, word of the earlier altercation had gotten out, and a couple of moms had come to have some words with us. One of these mothers I knew well—since I was a kid, in fact. She had lost her husband the month before and was taking it really hard. Needing backup, I sent for one of the community grandmothers, volunteering that day in the early childhood center, and she was quickly on the scene. Her calming effect was the miracle I'd been hoping for. Disaster avoided.

With 20 minutes to go before the morning break, I called my wife, Kathryn. Could she come over to help prepare food for the 90 kids in the school's feeding program? She was there a few minutes later, accompanied by Chef Ebony, our 4-year-old daughter, who messily and enthusiastically smothered jam onto slices of bread. The job got done.

By midday, the temperature was up over 100 degrees. With a new set of behavior issues to deal with, lunch for me was a fourth coffee and a week-old slice of birthday cake from the staff room fridge. I spent the rest of the afternoon immersed in one of my least favorite activities: conference calls with department staff, located anywhere from 300 miles away to more than 1,000.

At 2:45 the bell rang, and I leaned back in my chair, stretched my aching body, and rubbed my face roughly with my hands. My head was a throbbing mess of stress, exhaustion, and caffeine. As my vision came back into focus, I spied a small sticky note stuck to my computer monitor. In capital letters, it ordered me to GET OUT!—a blunt reminder that I needed to be out of the office and present in the learning and lives of my students and staff as often as I could be. I got out. I wasn't doing the afternoon bus run, but I wanted to say goodbye to as many of the kids as I could before they left for the day.

As they raced around the corridors of the school, I high-fived those nearest to me and yelled out to others.

"Awesome day today, Sarah! See you tomorrow!"

"Lucas, say hi to your pop and tell him I will see him at council tomorrow night."

"Maggie, same songs tomorrow morning on the bus! We'll see you early, hey? And make sure your brothers come with you this time."

Jess, my first passenger early that morning, ran up to me. "Hey, Mr. Faulkner, are we doing horse riding tomorrow?" she asked.

I knelt down, grinning from ear to ear. Jess had hardly missed a day since we launched the horse program, and after a weekend of brainstorming, she had decided to name the horse Jessie, after herself. She was crazy about that horse. "Yep, definitely, Jess," I replied. "Jessie will be pumped to see you." She raced off down the hallway, running her hands along the artwork that we had painted the term before with the help of some boys who had clocked hours in the juvenile justice system.

I headed down to the basketball court, eager for a few moments with the team. Their bare feet were slapping on the cracked concrete pavement. They were good—much better than me—and I quit after only a few minutes, the sweat already soaking my Halls Creek School T-shirt, the sun still high in the sky and burning hot.

In a day full of disruptions, the e-mails had been piling up in my inbox, and as the school quieted down for the day, I returned to my office to try to make a dent. The first e-mail was from a finance controller at the central office 1,500 miles away, asking me to explain why we had spent our behavior management grants in a way that was "unorthodox." In a moment of frustration, I deleted the e-mail...then immediately regretted it.

The next one was from a teacher whom I had spent the last seven weeks trying to recruit. She was an A-gamer –a passionate, highly skilled educator. We'd worked together two years before, when I held a different job. She was exactly what the Halls Creek team needed. The first lines of her message looked good. She talked about how she had loved working with me (very kind) and how she was honored that I had reached out to her. She recalled a few great moments from our old school. But then a single word in the second paragraph hit me like a ton of bricks: *sorry*. No, she could not accept a position. Her husband had just taken a mining job that the family couldn't refuse. I groaned quietly to myself, leaning my head against the screen.

In my short career, I'd built a reputation for resilience and getting the job done. A few colleagues at my first Principal's Association

Conference gave me the nickname "Mr. Fix-It." I had won a bunch of awards and been profiled often on national TV for the work I was doing in schools. But my place was not at award ceremonies or in front of cameras; my place was here, with the kids of Halls Creek, fixing things.

Today, though, Mr. Fix-It was failing. From the half-empty school buses to disrupted learning, from bloody fights to frustrated staff . . . I just wasn't in good form. Today, the job felt too big, too tough. I felt useless.

I was only 29 years old. Perhaps I was in over my head. Was it all worth it? Did anyone care? Were we making any difference at all? I thought about heading straight home to see Kathryn and the girls and to spend the rest of the afternoon just trying to be a better dad.

All this was interrupted by a knock on the door. I put on my game face and greeted my visitor. It was Robyn, our attendance officer.

I stood up and sat on the edge of the desk. I forced a smile. Robyn smiled back and her grin was wider than mine and genuine. She was waving a piece of paper in her hand.

"Mr. Faulkner, I'm here to make your day," Robyn said, bounding over to sit next to me. "I've got our official attendance numbers since we started the new 6-in-5 model."

Our 6-in-5 model was a bold attempt to squeeze six days of learning experiences into five days of school. It was a big swing for us, involving pulling in extracurricular activities beyond regular school subjects and giving students lots of ownership and authorship over what they learned, when they learned, and who was teaching them. The goal was to boost learning, engagement, investment—and yes, attendance.

I am a pretty optimistic person, but right then, I thought about all the empty seats on the morning bus run and prepared myself for underwhelming data. In my career, I had become used to big increases. I used to take great pleasure in drawing graphs with steep upward slopes—something I hadn't been able to do here.

"We have more students coming to school every day," Robyn beamed. "Way more, in fact! If you sum it up, more than 100 more students came to school for at least 95 percent of this term. Also—and this is absolutely fricking unheard of—more parents are bringing their children to school, which is why the buses are less full."

Robyn loved numbers, and she *really* loved these numbers. Her eyes were shining with tears.

I took a few seconds to respond, and the great lump in my throat allowed me only two words: "That's awesome." And then, against my wishes, tears came to my eyes as well.

Karen, one of my deputies, poked her head in the office. "You just told him, didn't you?" she asked, smiling. "It's amazing, right?"

All Robyn and I could do was sit there and nod, silly grins on our faces.

"I've got more news, though," Karen said, as she too hopped up onto the messy desk, squeezing between Robyn and me. She opened her laptop to a screen of literacy and numeracy test results and proceeded to decipher them for us, comparing the red squares splashed across the screen from last year with the green squares that showed how many kids were now on track. Then she opened an e-mail from the grade 10 teacher, which stated, with a healthy dose of exclamation marks, that *five* senior students were now in a position to take work placements, starting next semester. It was the impromptu meeting that I needed, from two people whose support I really needed.

A few hours later, as the sun began to set, I locked up the school and began the walk home. While there had been many tough days over the past year, I knew deep down that today was the first time I had thought about giving up. The school leader was supposed to be the strong one, showing the way for everyone else. Today, it was my team who had been there to pick *me* up, to get me through, to push our work forward. They were incredible people who gave the job everything they had.

Together, we were changing our school and doing great things for our kids, each other, and our community.

I knew there would be more tough days ahead, but with each step home, my resolve strengthened, my pulse quickened, and my smile widened. I even sent a quick text to Kate, apologizing again for cancelling today's training sessions and letting her know we'd figure out a way to fit them in tomorrow.

As I walked up the driveway to our little house, I saw the bus parked out the front, dropped off by my other deputy, Gary, after the end-of-school run. There was a note under the windscreen wipers: *Karen texted me about the results. So good!* I grinned as I folded it up, placing it into the pocket of my jeans. What a team we had.

A chorus of "Dad! Dad!'" and a rumble of footsteps greeted me, and soon my knees were wrapped up by the tiny arms of my daughters, Grace and Ebony, their school T-shirts covered in the red dust of Halls Creek. Our home.

why did we write *Dream Team*?

Years ago, at a TEDx conference afterparty, we—Aaron and Dave—hatched a plan on a napkin.

It was an audacious vision to help accelerate education change across the world.

At the time, Dave was working as a district superintendent. He had moved on from Halls Creek, but he was drawing on skills he had built there to help leadership teams in his region change their schools. Aaron had just returned from two years in Africa where he ran a school for street kids. Still thin from the multiple bouts of malaria he had contracted, he had started work on an organization that would back local teams of startup entrepreneurs in some of the world's poorest communities.

We discovered that we shared a few key beliefs.

We thought that the world could be a lot better than it was.

We thought that education was one of the fastest ways to drive positive change.

We thought that the pace of change in education could be accelerated.

We were also impatient and wanted to be part of helping make this happen *now*.

In the years since, the educator-led changes in education we have witnessed have been exciting. There are plenty of us working hard every day to prepare our kids for an increasingly uncertain world. We are staying up late thinking up ways to engage our students more deeply. We are learning, adapting, trying. We are making a difference.

As hungry as educators are for positive change, and as much as many of us love walking the aisles of education expos to see what innovative toys we can bring into our schools, living in today's state of flux can also leave us a bit flummoxed. Every day, it seems, we need to juggle curriculum changes, directives from the head office, and the latest research findings (which might just tell us that the new approach we've been piloting is, in fact, the opposite of what we should have been doing). Whenever we take a bold step forward with a new idea, we know that a step or two backwards might be just around the corner.

Yet we all show up for work each new day, walk into our classrooms and offices and staff rooms, and keep trying.

If this describes you, this book is *for* you.

It is for school leadership teams who are curious.

Who are hungry for change.

Who try to predict the future by having the courage to try to create it.

It was written by doers, about doers, and for doers.

It talks a little bit about why things should change and what needs changing, but it is mostly about *how to make change*. As Karl Marx said, "Philosophers have only interpreted the world in various ways. The point is to change it." (Yes, we just quoted Marx. It's a great quote, right?)

So the point of this book is to help leadership teams in schools change things.

Right about now, unless you are wondering if we are communists, you are probably asking yourself, "Aren't there already loads of books on education change?" The answer is yes, there are many (and no, we are not communists). You could fill a library shelf or a Kindle's hard drive with books on the subject. The great Michael Fullan has been releasing an excellent contribution every second year. His friend, the ever-friendly and big-brained Andy Hargreaves, has been almost as prolific, and occasionally they have even written together. John Hattie has delivered breakthrough ideas with his meta-analysis of thousands of research papers, as has his inspired compatriot, Viviane Robinson. And then there is Ken Robinson, who, in his charming way, has used his books and the TED Talk stage to challenge a generation of educators to do things differently while giving us a much-needed injection of optimism along the way. We have read the works of these experts and the works of many others, and we applaud them for their brilliant contributions.

We are a little different, though, and so is this book.

So, before we go any farther, who are *we*?

For a start, neither of us have the title "Dr." before our names. Aaron is the closest to having a PhD. Thanks to some academic overexuberance in his 20s, he collected a research MPhil from Cambridge and a few master's degrees from some other universities. He did this as a military officer bouncing between war zones and operations and then as a social entrepreneur while working in slums and villages in East Africa. Aaron went on to cofound an organization that has already helped to bring life-shifting changes to more than half a million people living in poverty.

Dave skipped out of university a year early and chose to finish his education degree on the job. After being selected for a rare school-based internship, he became a graduate teacher at 21, a principal at 24, and a district superintendent at 30. Throughout his career, he has led some of

Australia's most dramatic school turnarounds. Dave now advises governments around the world and speaks on the world's largest education stages about how other educators can lead change in their settings.

Seven years ago, we started an organization called Education Change-makers (EC), based on a simple idea: that the best ideas to change education almost always come from teachers and school leaders. While this seems like a pretty obvious concept, it's one we still feel we have to fight for, as far too many decisions about and directions for education are still being determined by those without a lived experience of the challenges of schools.

We assembled a team of brilliant education leaders from across the world, and the EC crew now work to support as many educators as we can by providing them with the tools to make change more effectively. Tens of thousands of people now come through our programs each year, and what they go on to do in their schools with the tools they acquire from us is astounding. We have witnessed good schools become great, dramatic rises in student engagement and learning outcomes, courageous moves into new pedagogies, brilliant implementations of new technologies, the launching of completely new schooling models, and exciting changes to the ways that educators come together to improve their schools and systems. Almost always, when these shifts have been schoolwide, they haven't come from one individual, or even from a particularly exceptional principal. They have come from a team of leaders—people with tremendous individual talents and strengths, who unite to achieve something truly extraordinary.

The parallel that jumps out to us was the U.S. men's basketball team at the 1992 Olympic Games in Barcelona—the famed "Dream Team" of NBA all-time greats, each at the peak of their powers. Ask anyone with even a passing interest in basketball to name some of the legends on this team, and you'll hear names like Michael Jordan, Magic Johnson, and Larry Bird. What was amazing about this group was that while individually they were all outstanding and the best players in their regular squads, together as one "Dream Team," they became the best basketball team the world had ever seen.

Yes, the world needs great individual education changemakers, capable of identifying problems worth solving, understanding those problems, finding innovative solutions, and scaling them for wide application; these are the "edupreneurs" we highlighted in our first book (Tait & Faulkner, 2016). But the world also needs *Dream Teams*—school-based, change-focused groups of talented administrators, teachers, staff, students, and community members who are passionate about making things better for kids, who believe that school-based change is the means to this end, and who are willing to roll up their sleeves and work together to make change happen.

This book is for Dream Teams in the making. It's a practical, real-world collection of stories and ideas designed to help you work together to change your school and systems faster and more effectively.

It sounds like our focus is transformational leadership, right? Well, yes and no.

We named our company Education Changemakers, and like Margaret Mead, we've never doubted that a small group of committed citizens can change the world. ("Indeed, it is the only thing that ever has.") So, it's interesting to us that *transformational leadership* has gotten a pretty bad rap from the education academics over the past decade.

In a 2007 research paper for the Australian Council for Education Research, Viviane Robinson reported that transformational leadership had an extremely modest effect on student achievement, only drawing an effect size of .14. Contrast that with .84—the gold-medal effect size of instructional leadership. While this finding is powerful, we have the niggling feeling that the breakdown of change in schools is often not so binary.

Admittedly, we have seen our fair share of leadership teams focus so much on transformational leadership that they failed to prioritize learning. At points in both our careers, we have been guilty of this. But we have also seen education leaders with a single-eyed focus on instructional leadership helm schools with terrible cultures, unhappy teachers, and a revolving door of personnel. The sweet spot, we think, is somewhere in between. When leadership teams who show many of the characteristics of transformational leaders channel their skills into bold efforts to lift teaching and learning, the results are a pleasure to see. This book attempts to find that line between transformational and instructional leadership.

It is also a book that we have tried to make as readable as possible—something you can get through in a few nights with a glass of wine in your hand or even while sitting on your favorite chair during the holidays. Although the book is underpinned by strong academic ideas, processes, and approaches (remember: Aaron has four degrees, one of them from Cambridge), we have not written it to be "academic."

how the book works

Dream Team is woven together out of three elements, reflecting the loosely controlled chaos that a change effort is.

About a third of the book is our insights and ideas. Thanks to extensive research and a wealth of experience, we have a strong sense of what school change looks like when it is led by a powerful leadership team.

Another third of the book is devoted to real stories of school change achieved by 10 brilliant leadership teams. We identified and spent time with these teams. The fiercely ambitious and inspired individuals that compose them didn't think in terms of how things were but of how things could be. Then they did the work to make those dreams come true.

You will meet the team from **Lesher Middle School** in the leafy suburb of Fort Collins, Colorado, and the team from **Jeremiah E. Burke Elementary School**, located in one of the most economically challenged parts of greater Boston. We'll take you to the Windy City and show you the powerful change being led by the team at **Chicago Tech Academy High**

School on the West Side. Then we'll head up north to dig into the successful change efforts that took place at **John A. Leslie Public School** and **John Polanyi Collegiate Institute**, both in the education powerhouse that is Ontario, Canada. After that, we will take you to the other side of the world—to our home country of Australia, where we'll look at how the team at Melbourne's **Wooranna Park Primary School** is striving to make a school that is "as exciting as Disneyland." We'll also learn from the team at **Cornish College**, a private school on acres of stunning wilderness, and go to the island of Tasmania to reflect on how the team at **Bayview Secondary College** fought to keep their school alive. Back on mainland Australia, in what might be the most isolated city in the world, we'll have a look at **Challis Community Primary School**, just a primary school on paper but so much more in reality. And then last but certainly not least, we journey to the homeland of John Hattie and Viviane Robinson to learn from the team at **Manurewa Intermediate School**, which is thriving in the center of one of New Zealand's most disadvantaged communities.

All these stories of leadership and change are brilliant, but that's all we'll say about them now—it would ruin the fun otherwise! As we move through the book and along the journey of change it presents, we will draw on these leadership teams' ideas, insights, and experiences to flesh out our own.

The final third of *Dream Team* provides real-world tools for innovation that you can take back to your schools and systems to help you change things faster and more effectively. We've called the whole book a "playbook" because what we present here isn't prescriptive. We lay out an approach and provide a variety of options that you might deploy, based on your school's challenges and the circumstances you find yourself in, to create the change you want to see. As the game changes, "Dream Teams" change with it and draw on other plays that they have up their sleeves.

We invite you to see us as your friends, fighting the good fight alongside you. We have been there ourselves (as have the leadership teams we profile), and we continue to work actively in schools and in disruptive education startups.

Have you ever been reading a leadership book that told you a practice you're using is absolutely the worst thing anyone could do? Have you had moments during a conference or a professional development session when the presenter rips a particular approach you're using to shreds, and you shrink into your seat thinking, *Oh, God, she's not talking to me, is she? Are people looking at me?* This book is not here to make you feel like that.

But it is not all pats on the back, either, because you won't get it right every time.

You will make mistakes. We all do. *Dream Team* is a manual to help you, and everybody else on your team, get it right more often. We've written it to help you figure out where your school is going, build the innovative culture to drive the solutions you need to that new reality, make what works stick, and then consider how the approach might be scaled and expanded to other schools so that even more kids can benefit.

We know that getting good at changing things can be quite hard to do without the right support and training. In business, many promising new leaders study for an MBA before they move into a role in the executive suite. In education, though, the system often plucks its best teachers from the classroom. Then, with relatively little training, these teaching stars are thrust into leading hundreds or sometimes thousands of people.

As the Swedish philosopher Bo Dahlbom said, "You can't do much carpentry with your bare hands, and you can't do much thinking with your bare brain. We need tools." This book gives you some of the tools you will need.

We have broken it down into an easy-to-follow, 10-step approach, which we call the Change Leader Journey (shown in Figure A). It's best implemented in the order we have laid out. Whenever you need to, you can pause or take a step back in the journey. You can certainly move through *Dream Team* all in one go, but know that it will come in handy at different stages of your change effort, so keep it close by for repeated reference.

Figure A

The Change Leader Journey

1. Passion
How can we start to build our Dream Team?

2. Listening
How can we source the right inputs to define the change ahead?

3. Focus
How can we focus on a few specific areas for change?

4. Alignment and Autonomy
How can we gain the confidence and authority we need to make the change we want to see?

5. Community
How can we best engage our community in this change?

6. Leadership
How can we enlist more leaders throughout the school to support this change?

7. Culture
How can we foster an innovative culture and generate new ideas for solving identified problems?

8. Solutions
How can we turn our innovative ideas into real change?

9. Proof
How can we prove our change initiatives have made the difference we hoped they would?

10. The Future
How can we make the change last . . . and what's next?

The Change Leader Journey is built on a focused analysis of what great teams are doing, distilled to the common threads and practicalities they used to make change happen in their school:

- Step 1 is to start with the heart, and that means determining (and juggling) what you want to value as a team. It's about bringing into account your various passions and beliefs, and then assessing your united commitment to the change effort ahead.
- Step 2 is to listen to your students, staff, and community members. Doing so dramatically increases the chances that you will build solutions that they feel are important.
- Step 3 is to determine the focus areas that your team will be working to solve.
- Step 4 is a balancing act—to align your approaches with the system while also forging the autonomy you need to be successful.
- Step 5 is to prepare your community for the challenging but purposeful days ahead.
- Step 6 is to tackle the challenge of distributing leadership across the school.
- Step 7 is to build a culture of innovation and leverage it to generate new ideas and solutions.
- Step 8 is to test and implement your solutions.
- Step 9 is to assemble your proof—sourcing the evidence you need to demonstrate your solutions' impact and prepare to embed them and increase that impact.
- Finally, there is Step 10, which is to keep the momentum up and make the improvements sticky, sustainable, and scalable before helping your team decide what work to tackle next.

Despite the challenge of educating students in and for this increasingly complex world, we are optimistic about the future. And we draw most of this optimism from people like you, passionate educators who are willing to forgive themselves every night and recommit every morning to making things better for kids. In the words of American transcendentalist and abolitionist Theodore Parker, famously paraphrased by Martin Luther King Jr., "The arc of the moral universe is long, but it bends towards justice."

Together, as a team, let's reach up, grab a hold of that arc, and pull it down toward better schools for the kids we teach.

1
PASSION

How can we start to build our Dream Team?

The year was 1968. On April 4, Martin Luther King Jr. was gunned down on a balcony in Memphis. Later that night, speaking from the back of a flatbed truck in Indiana, presidential candidate Bobby Kennedy asked those gathered to help "tame the savageness of man, and make gentle the life of this world." Two months later, he too would be killed.

Later that year, on a humid Boston morning, a 10-year-old Lindsa McIntyre packed her school bag and walked a mile from her home to Woodrow Wilson Elementary School. She was accompanied by her father, who had taken the morning off work, eager to support his daughter as she made the courageous step of being one of the first African American students in the city to be integrated into an all-white Boston public school. Lindsa was excited, too. Finally, she would see inside the kind of school that had been out of the grasp of so many Americans.

But Woodrow Wilson Elementary School didn't live up to Lindsa's expectations. When the winter arrived, she would find herself shivering in the unheated classrooms. She would find herself lined up with other students each morning to have her hair and fingernails inspected. Instruction was spartan, delivered in a strict and disciplined manner. But the greatest challenge for Lindsa was that, while her teachers meant well, they had very little understanding of what life was like for her and the other new, nonwhite children in their classrooms. They simply didn't know how to connect with the integrated students. "I loved school," Lindsa explained, decades later, "but I wasn't sure if school loved me."

Over the 1968–69 school year, 150 African American students joined the Woodrow Wilson school community. And an almost equal number of white students left, withdrawn en masse by their parents.

When Lindsa moved on to high school, things didn't improve. She and several other African American students did not attend any classes in the main building; they were sent to another building, three blocks away. They had no access to the gym, cafeteria, or nicer classrooms. Lindsa wanted more from her education, and for her life, but she felt trapped.

One evening after dinner she told her parents that she wanted to leave her high school. The news wasn't received well by her father, a man who worked long hours to feed his family of nine children. He argued that she should be grateful for the opportunity she had. But Lindsa was determined. She threw a challenge back to her father, inviting him to come with her to school the next morning and see what she was experiencing. So once again, as he had several years before, he took the morning off work and walked his daughter to school. They passed through the well-resourced main building, then out the doors and down the street to the annex area where the nonwhite students spent their days. Convinced, Lindsa's father gave her a task and the rest of the day to complete it. "Go home and look through the Yellow Pages," he said to her. "Circle three schools you want to go to, and tomorrow we will visit them all."

The next week, Lindsa started at Cambridge Academy, a small private school in very well-to-do Harvard Square. The school was exceptional, and Lindsa excelled there, working hard each day, acknowledging the sacrifices her parents were making to keep her there, even as the lights were turned off at home when power bills couldn't be paid. Years later, as a senior, Lindsa paid a visit to her old high school and was shocked by what she saw—shocked by the learning situation of her friends. Determined to pay her blessings forward, she began teaching them in her spare time. They thrived under her guidance, and Lindsa realized she had found her calling.

Her first official teaching job was at Jeremiah E. Burke High School, known locally as "the Burke." It's a four-story Art Deco schoolhouse built in 1934 and located in the Boston suburb of Dorchester. For Lindsa, it was the site of a hard-fought apprenticeship. She routinely found herself going above and beyond her regular lessons to engage with her students and attempt to understand the realities of their lives. Many of them were the children of Caribbean immigrants, and Lindsa tried to connect with them the way she wished her teachers back at Woodrow Wilson Elementary had done for her. She spent a decade at the Burke before moving on to pursue new challenges. Still, it felt to Lindsa like she was leaving part of her heart behind.

Decades later she returned to reclaim it. This time, as the headmaster. But the Burke was in trouble. A school of just over 500 students, it was averaging more than 500 suspensions a year. Only a third of kids were graduating, and only a fifth of the graduates were making it to college.

Within six months of Lindsa's arrival, the school was officially placed into turnaround. Yet Lindsa was as inspired as she had ever been. She believed she was in the right place, at the right time, and up to the challenge. She got to work building her team, and they rolled their sleeves up and changed the school.

assembling your dream team

Lindsa McIntyre has a powerful story. The image of her and her father walking into a newly desegregated school to help support a more united

United States is a stunning snapshot of a particular time and a place, reminiscent of the great Ruby Bridges only a few years before.

Lindsa's experiences made her the right leader for the Burke for many reasons, but here's what jumps out to us. First, she was a local. Lindsa had grown up in the greater Boston community, and she had even taught at the Burke before. Second, she had a lived experience of the problems she was trying to solve. Lindsa was uniquely placed to help the students at the Burke, because she had lived many parts of their stories herself. Third, she was passionate about making a difference at the Burke. And, as it turned out, she was going to need every ounce of that passion to help lead the change that would turn the school around.

While doing our research for this book, we spent a lot of time with a lot of school leadership teams and learned a lot about the people on them. Those three qualities of Lindsa's we just pointed out—local connection, lived experience, and passion—showed up again and again. They were so characteristic, in fact, that they are our foundational recommendations for assembling your Dream Team.

LOOK FOR LOCAL CONNECTIONS

Think back to Dave's story from his Halls Creek days. One of the most powerful assets he had up his sleeve was that his family had lived in the area for decades. The community elders were close friends of his parents and grandparents, and this engendered trust and gave him a certain standing. When Dave turned up as the principal, people were willing to listen to him.

We saw this same dynamic in so many schools:

- When Gill Berriman was appointed as the principal of Bayview Secondary College in Tasmania, she had been teaching at the school for 15 years. She was known, and she was respected.
- Being appointed as the principal of Manurewa Intermediate School in South Auckland was a homecoming of sorts for Iain Taylor. He had been a student there when he was 11 years old. His deputy

principal and right hand during the school's transformation was Greer Doidge. She had been at the school for 20 years.

- Local credibility was essential to pursuing change at Chicago Tech Academy High School. One of the reasons Principal Linnea Garrett and Assistant Principal Tiara Wheatley were taken seriously by the ChiTech kids and the community was that Tiara had grown up in the area and Linnea had spent the last 15 years of her career working in challenging schools on the South Side.

- Before coming to Lesher Middle School, Principal Tom Dodd had been working in Colorado as a teacher and athletics coach for 22 years. Deputy Principal Waren Morrow was a Fort Collins local who had served in the Colorado National Guard. Rounding out the team were teachers who were, respectively, a Fort Collins local and a 20-year Lesher veteran.

- The team of parents who led the change at Cornish College were local residents who had saved their hard-earned money to pay for a private education for their children. When they stepped up to lead, it was their friends, dinner party friends, and fellow book-club members whom they were mobilizing.

This is interesting to us. Often, the picture we have of a change agent, particularly in the corporate sector, is someone brought in from outside to kick some ass. No one within the community knows these people, and there is a great deal of fear around what they will do, whom they will fire, and how they will alter the culture. Yet in education, from what we have seen, the teams that are most effective at transforming schools have a heavy dose of local hometown heroes in their mix. So, if you are reading this book and feeling a little extra-confident right now because you have years of experience at the school or in your area, you're right to do so. Your change efforts just got a little power boost!

Not to say that it's impossible for an outsider, or an outside team, to make change happen; it just seems to be harder. And here, we are talking from experience. When Aaron was 25 years old, he was appointed as a school director for a very challenging school in Tanzania. He turned up with his wife, Kaitlin, a backpack of clothes, 20 words of Swahili, and a whole lot of passion. Here's is the briefing he received: "The school needs a lot of things to be fixed and some real leadership. Please bring it." Those of you who have read our first book, *Edupreneur*, know just how hard things got for Aaron, someone trying to lead change as an outsider. We will share some of these stories a little later for those of you we are just meeting now.

If you're not a local, if you're new to your community and can relate to Aaron in Tanzania with his 20 words of Swahili, you do have options, though. One way is to double your efforts to understand your community by listening, being conspicuous, and being present. Another is to lobby for adding more locals to your Dream Team right at this early phase of change. Look for leaders who have well-established credibility but also the openness to trying something new.

Whether a new leader is a born-and-bred local or an import, there is sometimes a tendency to come in and launch an overhaul of the school's entire leadership team, especially in a school that really needs some big changes. Our advice is to think carefully about this and not jump to conclusions about your legacy leaders. It is worth taking a little longer to figure out what different people may bring to the table. You may be pleasantly surprised by the assets you have—and by the positive contributions they can make. At Manurewa, for example, Iain Taylor found that he had, in Greer Doidge, a team member with deep connections to the community who was able to powerfully contribute to some of the school's most dramatic changes.

BRING IN AUTHENTIC UNDERSTANDING

When Lindsa McIntyre returned to the Burke as its leader, she brought a lived experience of the problems she was trying to solve. As a child, she had attended schools where staff struggled to empathize with the students in their classes who were "different" from themselves. She was well-versed in the challenges of poverty because she had lived through them herself, never forgetting the pangs of guilt she had felt when the electricity in her childhood home would be turned off (paying the bill came second to covering her private school fees). Where the majority of teachers would struggle to understand how a child feels in class the morning after witnessing a shooting on the streets or hearing the devasting news that a family member had been killed, Lindsa didn't. And because she knew the stories of the Burke's students so intimately, she was convinced that the traditional education approach that had been tried there for years was never going to succeed. She understood these kids needed something different.

Many members of leadership teams we spent time with for this book pointed to their past experiences—particularly their experiences as students—as heavy influences on their work. It's interesting that these experiences were generally negative ones. Aiman Flahat brought to his leadership role at John Polanyi Collegiate Institute the memory of being told that, as an immigrant to Canada, he should settle for second-best. He shared with us how, as a new arrival from Jordan, he sat down with the career advisor who immediately assigned him to the basic courses in the school rather than the advanced classes. When Aiman told his parents about this, his father was so outraged he went to the school the next day and demanded his child be placed in the advanced math and science courses. The following week, a frustrated career advisor told Aiman that he was fooling himself if he thought he could succeed in those classes. But succeed he did. Aiman graduated with honors and went on to study engineering and work on hydroelectrical plants. But he never forgot how little faith that teacher had in him. When Aiman kicked off the change effort at John Polanyi Collegiate, he did so with a fierce determination to provide every opportunity to every child. He vowed he'd never settle for anything less than high expectations in any school he was part of . . . and he did this because he understood what was at stake.

Digging down into your motivations to make a change in the world is an important and powerful thing to do. When Aaron met Nora Tager, an Ashoka fellow and accomplished social entrepreneur who has dedicated her life to social change in South Africa, he asked what kept her going through her struggles. The response he got from this little old lady, with her nice pearls, earrings, and well-pressed blazer, surprised him. "I harnessed the rage," she said.

Greg McLeod at John A. Leslie Public School is another who channeled his own disappointment with school into present, positive action. Greg grew up in a disadvantaged part of Toronto, and school for him was unengaging. He was more likely to skip school and get up to mischief with his friends than apply himself in class. It's probably not a coincidence that Greg focuses his leadership on making his schools as engaging as he can possibly make them. He understands what the alternative feels like.

As a leadership team, it is worth leaning in to your individual and collective motivation for undertaking change. *Why do you believe the things you do? Why are you the kind of educator you are?* In fact, *why are you an educator at all?* The greater your understanding of these points, the more likely you are to understand why you advocate for certain things for your students. And the better you understand your students, the more likely you are to advocate for what they really need.

PRIORITIZE PASSION

The task Lindsa signed up for was a mighty one: being the senior leader in a team charged with turning around one of the most challenged schools in the state of Massachusetts. She wasn't daunted, though; she was inspired. And this is the third thing that jumps out at us from her story as characteristic of so many change leaders we've met: they all had a huge passion to make a difference.

While this might sound a bit facile, we believe passion for the work is vitally important—so important that we want to talk more about it here, right at the beginning of the Change Leader Journey.

Changing a school, a learning culture, and often a community is serious work. Along the way you are going to upset a lot of people. You are going to find more gray hairs on your head than before you started. You will see less of your friends and family. You will start to get those physical ailments that come with stress. On a rare occasion, you might win an award that acknowledges what your team did. Or, even rarer but far sweeter, a student or parent will thank you for making the effort. But more often than not, you will be in the thick of a process that is messy and challenging—and is probably going to be so for years.

The quickest school transformation we saw during our research took place over three years. Most schools saw core members of their leadership teams buckling in for about seven years, about the same time as a two-term president of the United States. We don't want to scare you, but take a look sometime at the "before" and "after" photos of the past few U.S. presidents. It will give you a sense of what you're signing up for.

There's no getting around it: if you want to be part of a team that will lead a powerful change in your school or learning community, you need to commit to investing the time that change requires. You need to be able to give it your all, which means you need to come in wanting this badly. You must have a passion for the work. As Steve Jobs once said, "You have to be burning with an idea, or a problem, or a wrong that you want to right. If you're not passionate enough from the start, you'll never stick it out."

Almost all the principals we spent time with while researching this book fought hard to win the roles at their schools. Eight of the 10 left very comfortable jobs at well-functioning schools to take on the role of leading a transformation effort. Many of the deputies and assistant principals we spent time with had turned down multiple job offers with higher pay and greater seniority at other schools so they could stay the course with their current team.

We also found it interesting that these leadership teams took a while to lock in. At the very beginning of the change effort, there was a period where the existing members of the leadership team, as individuals, had to ask themselves a tough question: *Were they really willing to give all that was required?* Showing great honesty and professional integrity, some people acknowledged that they were tired, overextended, and out of ideas. They chose to move to other schools or to step out of a leadership role and focus on classroom work. Occasionally, members of these teams would have the gumption to challenge fellow members in whom they lacked confidence, and some of these discussions made the challenged individuals understandably upset.

But surprisingly, when challenged, most people rose to the occasion. For example, soon after his arrival at Manurewa, Iain Taylor began an audacious effort to rapidly refresh his leadership team. He wanted to bring in new people—professionals he trusted and had worked with before. But Greer Doidge, a local with 20 years of experience at the school, dug in her heels. She wasn't going anywhere except along for the change journey. Greer's passion for her school, her staff, and her kids made her a powerful and often counterintuitive voice on the team.

We recommend that right now, here at the beginning, you and every member of your team take a moment to reflect honestly on how inspired and ready you are to move into a period of transformation and hard work. There are plenty of ways that you can do this, but one that we have found useful is to actually plot your levels of inspiration and effectiveness across your career. Get it out on paper, noting different phases of your practice or positions you've held, thinking about your best moments, your worst, and where you are now. We've provided an example in Figure 1.1—a map of Dave's career in action. Notice his frustration during university and the love for school leadership that emerged during his first principal job. (For Dave, the toughest jobs are generally the most inspiring.)

On your team, how have individuals' inspiration levels changed throughout their careers? What were the circumstances in which you felt most and least passionate about the work? Most and least effective? How have internal and external challenges affected your inspiration and effectiveness? What about shifts in leadership and organizational goals?

Figure 1.1

A Sample Map of Personal Inspiration and Effectiveness

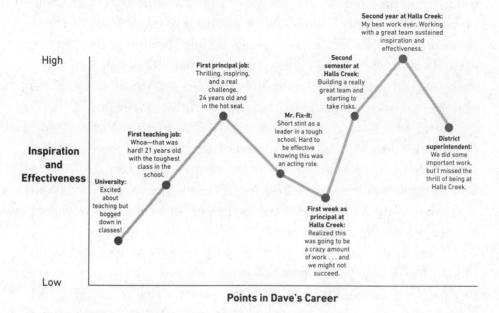

We hope that your team has the kind of culture that allows everyone to feel safe sharing these insights openly. (If you do, please be as honest as you can, and don't plot your current passion level score higher or lower than it really is.) As a group, it can be really powerful to dig into these results. The big question to answer is whether you collectively—this particular grouping of leaders—are ready for the period of change ahead.

If you are brave, before you start discussing team members' various passion levels, ask each member of the team to give their thoughts on what the overall team passion ought to be. This little activity may provide a quick win –a chance to confirm that you are all ready to go—or it may catalyze a few tough conversations about whether you really have the right people you need.

RECOGNIZE ONE ANOTHER'S PASSIONS

Passion is not a one-dimensional human experience, and chances are that the different members of your team are inspired by different things. Some people have a real passion for finding solutions to problems, so engaging in these early phases of school change will be something that they are excited about. Others find great purpose in helping people and will be energized by the thought of supporting teachers working to improve their practice, assisting students to engage powerfully in learning, or reaching out to parents to change a community. Consider too that in a world where loneliness, depression, and anxiety are becoming more prevalent, and where many of us are more connected to our personal devices than human community, there will likely be people on your team who are passionate simply about the idea of being part of a collective working to achieve something great.

A framing device we have found helpful is psychologist Robert Vallerand's (2010) model of harmonious versus obsessive passion. According to Vallerand, harmonious passion is the one to strive for. People working within harmonious passion are highly engaged in their work because it brings them intrinsic joy. When your work is aligned with your value system, there are huge benefits, including improved physical health, self-esteem, creativity, flow, and work satisfaction. Obsessive passion first may seem quite similar, but if you dig a little deeper, it is often more about achievement—one person trying to prove himself or herself right, prove someone else wrong, or just win. This model explains why many successful sports coaches often rely on a simple mantra to have their athletes perform as well as possible: *Push away the noise and just have fun out there.* People displaying signs of obsessive passion often confess that they can't stop thinking about work and that it forms a large part of their self-concept; this is correlated with increased chances of negativity, burn-out, and higher aggression. These quick insights underscore how valuable it is to recognize what kinds of passion you have on your team and how that can affect individual and collective behavior.

RAISE PASSION LEVELS

If you are lucky, you will be in a position where your entire team is passionate (ideally with harmonious passion) and ready to go for the change chapter that lies ahead. But this is not always the case, and rather than glossing over these realities, this is a vitally important time to discuss them. Maybe as you engaged as a team, some of you admitted to being tired, to having lost that loving feeling. Or maybe, while people weren't admitting it, others could tell that they were not as sharp as they once were. This is all totally normal, and to be expected, because the work you do as educators is hard, very hard.

But rather than just giving up or moving people on, there is plenty that we can do to try to raise the levels of inspiration and effectiveness to their once-high places. The first is to tap into the power of purpose, and the Japanese have a very useful concept for this called "ikigai." While much has been written on ikigai, a 2016 book by Francesca Miralles and Hector Garcia is a friendly introduction to the idea. Literally, *ikigai* means "a reason for being"; more colloquially, it means the reason one gets up in the morning. To find your ikigai, you draw four overlapping circles, one for what you love, one for what you are good at, one for what you can actually be paid to do, and one for what the world needs. What lies in the middle is your ikigai. If your being in the particular school you are in and doing the particular work you are doing is your ikigai, brilliant. If not, it may be time to consider either how you spend your time in the school or whether this school or this specific job is right for you.

Another approach that can help raise teamwide levels of inspiration and effectiveness is to increase the autonomy members have. Quite simply, the more autonomy people have in their own work and efforts, the more likely they are to be inspired by their work. As Steve Jobs once famously said, "It doesn't make sense to hire smart people and then tell them what to do; we hire smart people so they can tell us what to do." Jobs, an often-aggressive taskmaster, was famous for spotting supremely talented people and then getting the best out of them. For example, he was certainly not the lead founder of the iPod; that's a title better ascribed to Jon Rubinstein. Similarly, it was Jonny Ive, not Jobs, who was the creative force behind the company-saving iMac computer. This is a reminder that if passion levels aren't quite where you need them to be for the change chapter ahead, you might consider giving key members of your team more impressive job titles and more power to determine where the school is going and how it is going to get there.

But now let's jump into checking whether the members of your team are passionate about the same things and sufficiently aligned to be willing to solve the same problems.

aligning team passions

While it is too early in the transformation effort to determine exactly what the change effort's strategic priorities and activities will be, it is still important to get a sense of the approaches and beliefs of the leadership team as a whole. Simply put, a leadership team that has misaligned priorities will be building on a poor foundation.

When we spent time in the schools we profiled in this book, we saw leadership teams whose passions were unified and explicit:

- At Wooranna Park Primary School, the team was focused on making learning as engaging as possible.
- At the Burke, the team was committed to supporting the whole child, no matter how challenging the child's situation.
- At ChiTech, the team was driven by the belief that powerful and deep learning is possible for all kids.
- At John A. Leslie, the team believed that every child could be a changemaker.
- At Lesher, the team was committed to offering an elite learning experience that all children could access.

These kinds of powerful statements of passion are absolutely informed by strategic priorities, but there is little doubt that the personalities and personal passions of individuals on each leadership team played a part in shaping those priorities. For example, Tom Dodd, principal of Lesher Middle School, worked as an elite wrestling coach, and in that role, he was always pushing the members of his team to meet high expectations. Principal Ray Trotter of Wooranna Park made international headlines for expressing his belief that school should be "as exciting as Disneyland" and for his commitment to physically constructing engaging learning environments, by hand, often over the school holidays. The ChiTech team became extremely inspired by deeper learning approaches, particularly those displayed by High Tech High School, even before Linnea Garrett assumed the principalship. She was brought in on this wave of change, quickly harnessed the passion of her fellow leaders, and applied it to get real results.

The first step in bringing team members' various passions into alignment is to clarify what those passions are. What education topics are folks reading about? What do they get excited to see on the program at educational conferences? What approaches are they bringing up in the staff room? What are they evangelizing about and continually trying to implement or work toward? The quickest and easiest way to sort through this information is to have each person finish this sentence: "What *I* think we should be doing for our students is _____."

The aim here is to summarize big ideas into some bullet points or short sentences so you can move more quickly toward alignment. For example, one member of your team may say, "What I think we should be doing for our students is ensuring that that their teachers are as good as they can be." Another might say, "What I think we should be doing for our students is making sure they have the capabilities they need to thrive in the future." Capture all these passion statements on a big sheet of poster board or in a projected document, and see if you can whittle it down to three areas that you are united behind. While these are not the strategic directions the school will necessarily take (these will come later), it is important to determine whether you are on similar pages as a leadership team.

As your team works to clarify your various personal passions and align them into a unified commitment, take note of whether you're leaning toward more traditional priorities and approaches or whether you're drawn to the cutting edge. If they are more traditional approaches, be sure to "future-proof" them by ensuring that they will provide students with the capabilities needed in a rapidly changing world. If it is new approaches that excite you, be sure to seek out and stay abreast of the emerging evidence of their effectiveness.

So that is Step 1 of the Change Leader Journey.

Drawing on Lindsa McIntyre's story, we saw that the most powerful change leaders often work in teams with a healthy blend of locals who have powerful connections in their community. There are people on the team who have a lived experience of the problem they are trying to solve, which brings huge empathy to the task at hand. The team members share a high level of passion for the same kinds of work and are buckled in for the long-term commitment necessary to make this transformation happen.

A leadership team that takes an honest look at itself now is much better positioned to take on the work of the next stage, when team members must park their own ideas for a period and listen to the ideas of others in their school and community.

2
LISTENING

How can we source the right inputs to define the change ahead?

Opening Your Ears Can Open Your Eyes

Aaron Tait

Dar es Salaam, Tanzania, 2007

I left my job of seven years as an officer in the military, and my wife, Kaitlin, and I sold most of what we owned, handed back the keys to our rented apartment, and took a one-way flight to East Africa. We spent three months as humanitarian aides in Kenya at a time when the country was experiencing the worst violence it had seen in decades. Then we moved to Tanzania to lead a secondary school for street kids.

Kaitlin and I settled into the township that was to be our new home and got to work. Every morning we would wake up with smiles on our faces, make a pot of strong black coffee, blast local tunes over our cheap little radio, and get inspired for a day trying to bring change to a bunch of kids who really needed it. We set some big goals—the biggest being getting at least 10 of the school's senior kids through the national exams and into university. In a school where only one student had achieved this in the three previous years, the odds were against us.

Our five bouts of malaria within the first six months made an already tough job even tougher. We were also subjected to investigations from the police (who suspected we were CIA) and continual threats from an inhospitable mayor. I heard that underperforming staff members would use their final paycheck to pay the local witch doctor to put a curse on me.

When Kaitlin and I had been in Tanzania for almost a year, my parents came to visit. They saw how we were living, sat us down, and told us how worried they were that we were going to die in the township. My parents were passionate, compassionate, and well-traveled global citizens, but they found it hard to understand why we were pushing so hard and willing to sacrifice so much of ourselves.

But we knew our why.

We loved the kids in the school, and we were fighting for a new future for them. And in a community where it was estimated that two in five people had HIV/AIDS, and four in five kids didn't finish high school, a new future was certainly needed.

One afternoon, when Kaitlin and I had been at the school for six months, I was marking some assignments in the little shack that we called home, which was just inside the school fence. One of the teachers (in fact, the only other teacher left beside ourselves) walked past the front door, on his way home after his final class for the day. I asked him in for a cup of tea, hoping to inspire him with a little pep talk. His name was Anthony, and he was a brilliant teacher—a local guy who had grown up tough but made it through school and now wanted to help the next generation.

As I made a tea for Anthony, I started to talk. "You have been amazing, my friend, and I feel like we are really making progress here," I began. "I know things are tough, but I feel like if we can just push that little bit harder this month, the kids will see the progress they are making, and we will be on track to getting a load of them through their exams."

His response was not what I was expecting.

"Aaron, you need to take a break," Anthony said.

"I didn't come here to take breaks," I replied. If my seven years in the military had taught me one thing, it was resilience. We were going to get this job done.

"No, Aaron—honestly," he said. "You need to get away."

I turned around and smiled, but then I saw the fear in his face. "I overheard some of the boys talking about you this afternoon," he continued.

"OK, I'd love to hear it," I said. "Then let's fix it and move on."

"Aaron, it's really bad," Anthony said. "In a few hours, these boys are going to come to your house, and they are going to kill you in front of your wife."

This stopped me in my tracks. The threat was real, very real, and this was not the kind of place where the police could come to the rescue or a counselor could be called in from the head office. There were no protocols for something like this, and I had to think quickly.

As a reader and an educator, I'm sure you have some theories about what I could have done or should have done. But what I did as a 25-year-old trying to make a difference in a very tough place was this— and it's not a course of action I would recommend for anyone else.

First, I asked Anthony to look out for Kaitlin—to get her here, into our house, as soon as school finished and to get her somewhere safer if things went bad. Then I thanked him and walked outside, back toward the classrooms. I passed Kaitlin in the square and gave her a kiss on the cheek. I told her Anthony was looking for her and wanted to discuss his lesson plans. When I spotted one of the student leaders, I asked him to gather as many of the boys as he could and meet me in one of the classrooms.

I sat there silently as the boys began to stream in, glancing around at the class that we had built together. After 50 or so boys had filled the classroom, I asked one at the back of the room to pull the door shut.

I stood up in front of them, took a deep breath, and said, "The rumor is that you want to kill me tonight. Well, I don't want Kaitlin to see it happen, so . . . if you're going to kill me, do it right now."

Then I waited for them to rush me. Just a month prior, a teacher at a school a few miles away had been killed by his students.

None of my students moved.

I should have been frightened, but honestly, what I felt most in those moments was frustration, confusion, and anger. So I challenged them again. "Come on!" I said. "We talk about being men of courage, men of honor. If you really want to do this, this is your chance."

But still none of them moved.

And at that moment, my bravado fell away, and I realized how wrong I had been. Not just on this day, but on all the days before.

I had come to this township to "fix" it. I was convinced that I had the answers to change the school. I felt so sure that so long as I led that school with everything I had, and so long as I never gave up on the kids, I would make their futures better.

I had all the right intentions but the wrong approach.

So I apologized.

"*Pole sana,*" I said. "I am so sorry." And I meant it. The tears in my eyes gave it away.

At the school, we could only afford one stick of chalk each week, but right then, I handed the chalk to the boy closest to me. Then I asked the rest of the students to tell him everything that I had done wrong as a leader. I sat quietly on a stool at the side of the room and listened as they detailed all my failures. I watched the board fill up with chalk. It took three hours.

At the core of it all, though, was a very simple message that I needed to hear: *Aaron, what you were doing was your vision, not ours.*

To be honest, this was tough to hear. When Kaitlin and I arrived six months earlier, we had been shocked by the condition of the school and the community. Bear in mind that as a military veteran and someone who had traveled to more than 50 countries by then, I wasn't easy to shock.

With my failures thoroughly documented and the students' message finally clear to me, my response was to do something very simple.

I asked them to tell me about *their* vision for the school.

I asked them to write the kind of rules they would like to see—rules for both students and teachers.

I asked them how they wanted to learn.

I asked them what success would look like by the end of the year.

And I was shocked once more by their responses. The students set more ambitious targets and higher expectations than I ever had. They were willing to work hard, but they needed a say in it.

On that day, those kids taught me more about leadership than my time at the military academy or Cambridge University ever did. My new mantra—the idea that has defined the organizations I have started and the teams I have led ever since—became this: *The only thing more powerful than ownership is authorship.* And that is what this chapter, and this step in the Change Leader Journey, is all about. How to listen for what you really need to hear. How to let your kids, staff, parents, and community inform your leadership team's plan for change.

some ground rules for change-focused listening

In the film *Up in the Air*, George Clooney plays a man named Ryan Bingham, a carry-on-suitcase-wheeling, perfectly trimmed, tailored-suit-wearing "corporate downsizer." He flies around the United States, walks into boardrooms, fires people, and "saves" the companies.

If we are honest with ourselves, some new leaders are tempted to be a little like Ryan Bingham. When we are brought into schools that need change, or when we assemble as a team with a mandate to get things done, we know that the status quo won't shift anything. Being nice to everyone won't get much done either. As a military officer, Aaron was trained and expected to walk into situations of disorder, sometimes literally with bullets flying, and bring order quickly. If he couldn't do that, the superior officers would find someone who could. Perhaps this is why, in Tanzania, he initially led the way he did.

Greg McLeod admits to leading like this during his first year as principal at Toronto's John A. Leslie Public School. He didn't fire staff, but he did write his own plan that he was sure would succeed. He had been lecturing on education at a prestigious university for the prior three years, and he drew on contemporary research and theories to compose an instructional leadership approach targeting writing improvement. "I was going to be the instructional leader that came in with best practice and moved the numbers quickly," Greg said.

The plan looked great on paper, excited his system leaders, and would have impressed Greg's fellow academics back at the university, but in the real world of John A. Leslie, it didn't work. "No one owned this plan," Greg admitted. In many ways, he confessed, that first year was a wasted year. But it was an important lesson that forced him to get over his feeling that he had the answers.

Greg needed to look up from the books and look outward to his staff, students, and community members. He needed to listen to what they had to say.

So we're all in agreement that listening to your people is important, but we have two ground rules your team needs to grasp before we go any further.

DON'T LISTEN FOR TOO LONG

At some point, you need to thank everyone for their insights and start figuring out what you are actually going to do in the real world. There is a time and a place to be a psychologist listening to people share on your couch, and a time and place to be the builder who gets things done. Be sure to keep an ear out to gain feedback on how things are going, but have the courage to implement what you decide to do based on what you are hearing and what you have heard.

DON'T EXPECT THAT LISTENING WILL BE ENOUGH

Listening is about soliciting insights, not getting an entire game plan. As Henry Ford is supposed to have said, "If I asked people what they wanted, they would have said faster horses." Hear what people are telling you, think carefully about what it means, and use it to move forward. In Tanzania, for example, Aaron was still a key leader in the school, but he and his team decided to heavily inform their approaches with student-generated insights.

getting the input you need

Now it's time share some of the listening strategies we picked up from our Dream Teams.

USE SURVEYS

Iain Taylor surveyed students, staff, and community members widely before he even started the job as principal of Manurewa Intermediate School. He chose to make the surveys anonymous, because he loved how honest people were willing to be when they were not fearful of saying the wrong thing. As Iain read through the responses, he searched for key trends rather than outlier opinions. That was a wise approach. Think of how it's usually more helpful to read all the three- and four-star reviews of restaurants you're considering rather than aggressive one-star reviews. The latter tend to be written by people we sometimes refer to as "happiness vacuums," capable of sucking the positivity out of any room they walk into!

At Lesher Middle School, Tom Dodd and the rest of the leadership team embraced the anonymous survey approach too, continually reaching out to their school community with anonymous surveys, monitoring feedback, and never resting on their laurels. As Tom put it, "We are always surveying, tracking, and digging into parent perceptions. Students complete perception surveys about their teachers. We have a climate and culture survey, where there are specific questions about how our leadership team is performing. I take these surveys very seriously."

Survey data are only as good as the surveys that generate the data. You need honest input and a sufficient response rate to draw valid conclusions. Therefore, the first practical matter is to make sure your surveys are carefully constructed—and not boring or too long. At our organization, EC, we have achieved dramatic increases in survey completion rates by deliberately making our surveys as engaging as possible. A favorite strategy is to take the time to give life to response options. This sees us swapping out questions like . . .

On a scale of 1–5 (with 1 being the low response), how would you rate the culture at this school?

low response	1	2	3	4	5	high response
	○	○	○	○	○	

. . . for something a little more fun:

How would you rate the culture of this school?

○ To be honest, I prefer the dentist.

○ I have moments of quiet desperation as an employee here, but with counseling, I am getting through.

○ It is a mixed bag—kind of like a family gathering where you like some of the cousins, but there are definitely a few cousins to avoid.

○ This school is great. People are friendly, and we work hard. One gold star.

○ You could give me a million dollars and I'd still be here on Monday!

Surveys can also feel awkward for some staff members, even threatening. A simple way to reduce the fear of recrimination is to ensure responses are anonymous; people are more likely to tell you what they really think when they're sure they won't suffer for their honesty. Also, don't share all the comments and scores publicly. Instead look for key trends and shield staff from statements made about them that are rude and could cause offense. Insights are great; nervous meltdowns from staff members are not.

WALK AROUND

As we mentioned in the opening story, when Dave was a principal, he had a sticky note on the side of his computer that had two words on it: *Get Out!* He might not have an MBA, but as a school leader, he used to follow the "MBWA" theory: "Manage By Walking Around."

At John Polanyi Collegiate Institute in Toronto, newly hired principal Aiman Flahat found himself working over the Christmas holidays in the wake of a burst water pipe. He spent four days largely alone in the building, trying to relocate classrooms and resources. Walking the empty corridors, he saw a school that was down on its luck with plenty of things in need of repair. He spent two weeks of his holidays coming in alone to clean, fix, and prepare the school for a new future. Aiman hadn't even met his fellow leaders yet, but he was racking up interesting insights every day.

A few suburbs away, at John A. Leslie Public School, Principal Greg McLeod was also walking the halls—or in his case, traversing the levels of the school. "I saw a really interesting physical space, which gave me insights into what was happening culturally," he said.

The school had been built in seven different sections over decades. This meant that as people moved through the space, they needed to go up and down sets of stairs into different areas that looked and felt misaligned. It struck Greg that John A. Leslie "was actually just a collection of pods of teachers, working in silos, and not a whole school." The leadership team used this insight to set a new goal: *Be as conspicuous as possible.* Visual team unity was a way to communicate to staff that all of the leaders were on board with making the entire school more effective.

In Colorado, the leadership team at Lesher Middle School also decided to make themselves very conspicuous, regularly attending weekend sporting events in Lesher Vikings T-shirts and getting around the campus to talk to parents and kids. At the beginning of the school day, Principal Tom Dodd stands outside to greet the students as they stream out of yellow school buses and SUVs or chain up their bikes. He confessed he hadn't taken a sick day since he joined the school.

Sometimes leadership teams are able to deduce trends from time spent listening and observing. And sometimes, the insights come immediately, as subtle as an uppercut. Ray Trotter from Wooranna Park Primary School still remembers a student telling him that, at home, he spent 95 percent of his time on his passion, but that at school, he never got any time to work on it. Statements like this inspired the Wooranna Park leadership team to try to make their school the most engaging place their students have ever seen.

Similarly, back in Toronto, Aiman casually mentioned to a student that the hooded sweatshirt the boy was wearing made him look like a gangster. The boy looked at Aiman, who was wearing a well-tailored suit, and replied, "Actually, the biggest criminals all dress like you." Instant insight. Aiman resolved right then to never again pass quick judgment on his students or rush into forcing his norms onto them.

Is your leadership team sufficiently present in your school? Are you out and about, and are you truly listening? If you're listening, what are you learning?

PAY ATTENTION TO NARRATIVES

Another interesting technique used by the Dream Teams was how they considered the narratives surrounding the school when formulating change strategies. Very early in their work, they tried to find out what the school was known for. Did it have a nickname that it couldn't shake, for better or worse? What were parents saying about the school? What were staff in the feeder schools saying to parents about it? These intangible shapers of culture, which can only be ascertained by honestly and authentically reaching out to people for insights, can be very powerful.

At one of Dave's schools, he spent the weekend before his official first day as principal chatting with the grandmothers in the community— women who trusted him because of his strong family ties in the town. When Dave asked them what they thought about the school, he got the same message from all of them, and it was loud and clear: "That place is not safe for our kids." It was a heartbreaking thing to hear, but it was a key insight that helped guide the leadership team's work.

Narratives shape experiences. When we drove around Fort Collins, a college town in Colorado, we felt like we were seeing the America we knew from sitcoms and films. There were U.S. flags planted in well-tended front lawns. There were children cycling to school down tree-lined streets, pausing at traffic lights to allow yellow school buses to drive past. Yet when we asked any member of the leadership team at Lesher Middle School how the school was perceived by the people of Fort Collins a decade ago, they all said the same thing: "We were known as the ghetto school." Fort Collins is a long way from the ghetto, and the staff know this. When they told us this story, they all either smiled ruefully or shook their heads. As far from the truth as the label was, it still had an impact.

And sometimes it is what you see, more than what you hear, that can help leaders to understand the public perception of their organization. Case in point is a key cultural fable that's become part of the folklore of Samsung, a company with revenue representing 17 percent of the gross national product of South Korea. Back in 1993, Samsung chairman Lee Kun Hee traveled around the world to see how his products were doing. In Southern California, he strolled into an electronics store and saw his competitor's TVs were in prime positions, spotlighted and on display for customers. His company's products were in a far corner, gathering dust. This told Lee in no uncertain terms that he needed to shake things up, so he brought his entire team together for a historic meeting where he implored them to "change everything but their wives and children." (We certainly hope Samsung has since done some work to increase gender diversity at its leadership level.)

What might your leadership team learn by spending some time listening to what people are saying about the school? What signs might you pick up about how your school is perceived or valued or not valued at all?

When Aaron was a humanitarian worker in Kenyan villages, he would spend at least one day a week on his bicycle cycling around to different communities, talking with the grandmas (much like Dave used to do). Their insights would give him a sense of why kids were dropping out of school, getting into trouble, or not visiting the health clinics. As is Kenyan custom, every chat was accompanied by a shared flask of chai, a sweet tea made with fresh milk from the family cow. One cup of chai was nice;

20 cups in a single day was overwhelming and led to frequent bathroom stops on the ride home. But all that tea Aaron drank was a sign that he had been listening. Beyond the questions he asked, he rarely spoke in those meetings. Every time he felt like he wanted to jump in or defend what his organization was doing when people weren't happy with it, he would take a sip of tea or ask another question.

The leadership team at John Polanyi Collegiate went out of their way to listen to parents, particularly in the early days when they were trying to get a sense of what needed changing. Aiman told us this:

> Parents were very upset, and I had to listen and not be defensive. It takes a lot to really listen and to not be upset when someone is yelling at you, and they want something, and you know that, for now, you are unable to deliver it. But you need to be able to tell them how glad you are that they are so passionate about their children's future. We want parents to advocate for their children, which is so much better than them not caring.

The team at Jeremiah E. Burke High School took the same approach, consuming many cups of coffee that summer before their first full school year as leaders. Principal Lindsa McIntyre recalled spending every weeknight at a different parent's house. "Half of them thought I was crazy," she laughed. "It was just something so new for them." These visits were really simple. The Burke leaders would make a simple request: "Tell us about your child and tell us what you think the school should be doing for them." Then they would listen, intently. Similarly, at Challis Community Primary School in Western Australia, members of the leadership team started conversations with this question: "If I were a fairy godmother, what would you want me to do for your child?"

The insights Lindsa and the Burke team gained during their fieldwork on those warm Boston nights helped them shape the innovations of the next few years. In fact, home visits were such a powerful strategy that they became a standard part of transition: all rising freshman students receive at least one visit from school leaders in the summer before their first semester. These home visits also informed a unique offering that the Burke team would go on to create: night classes for parents and caretakers on topics ranging from technology to well-being, all designed to reinforce the belief that what Burke was doing with their children was powerful and worthy of their support.

SCRUTINIZE THE NUMBERS

At Challis Community Primary School, "the numbers" heavily inform almost every major decision the leadership team makes. When Lee Musumeci started as principal, there was one indicator that jumped out at her, and it became a linchpin for the interventions that the team would go on to build. Only 29 percent of Challis's arriving 5-year-old preprimary students were reading at state level, and by the end of their first year, the number was only marginally higher, at 39 percent. Quite simply, children were coming to school underperforming, and, despite the best efforts of the school's team, most of them were not catching up.

Many of the leadership teams profiled in this book could recite a similar set of key numbers that heavily influenced the decisions they made together. Literacy and numeracy scores are, of course, commonly referenced by teams from primary schools and secondary schools, particularly in the United States. Suspension rates are often referenced by schools that are struggling to cope with behavior (such as the Burke, which one year reported more than 500 suspensions in a student body that itself was just over 500 strong). Graduation and student destination data are also very common across school types, but the most basic number of all, mentioned even by well-funded private schools, is enrollment totals.

It is vitally important that a leadership team doesn't shy away from these numbers at the beginning of a transformation effort. Be aware that this will hurt, particularly for those who have been at the school as leaders during a period of poor outcomes. But, as the saying goes, surgeons must wound before they heal. Digging into the data and being honest about them is literally like slicing open the school and getting a sense of what's really happening inside. Numbers don't tell the entire story, but they certainly give us a critical part of it.

LISTEN UNTIL ACTION MAKES SENSE

We have already advised you not to listen for "too long," so how long should you listen before you act? Honestly, it depends on your team. If you are a team full of Type-A personalities, it's likely you'll want to jump in right away and start solving problems. And that's fine.

Iain Taylor at Manurewa in New Zealand took this approach. He surveyed staff and some students, assessed the numbers, and then, during his interview for the principal job, presented a bold plan he called "Countdown 75." Believing that the school needed a fast and conspicuous change of course, he took total leadership very quickly, set new standards, and initiated rapid changes that would all be achieved within 75 days. The plan was short and easy to understand. The leadership team followed up with "Rocketing 290," which guided the work for the remainder of the year. This second plan was heavily informed by insights Iain and his reinvigorated leadership team gained during their first three months.

But just across the water in Tasmania, Gill Berriman took a totally different approach. At her first interview for the principal position at Bayview Secondary College, Gill's system leaders asked about her plan to change the school. Her response was brief and reflected her leadership style perfectly. "I don't have a plan yet," she said. "I need to listen to everyone first." A few days later, she was politely informed that she wouldn't be going through to the next phase. But then, a few days after that, they invited Gill back in, this time asking explicitly for her to present a plan. Seven years later, she is cheeky enough to admit, "I made up a plan to keep them happy, knowing full well that it was all likely to change once I had the chance to truly listen to the thoughts of everyone that I wanted to chat with."

And listen she did . . . for almost an entire year. Bayview students were not performing well, but Gill was eager to value everyone's efforts. She had cups of tea with every member of staff. She spent months collating data. She sent out multiple rounds of surveys to stakeholders and didn't allow herself to be discouraged when a survey received just six parent responses. Gill devoted afternoons to catching up with the charismatic manager of the child and family center, who was on top of all the gossip swirling around the community. She returned multiple times to the feeder schools, asking them to tell her honestly how they were supporting their students' transition into her school. The insights she gained were varied and many, but by the start of the next school year, Gill's leadership team had a plan.

So there you see the two extremes. One leader who wrote a plan before he even had the job, and another who spent a year listening, learning, and preparing before she was ready to truly write hers. Where will your team sit between these two approaches?

preparing for action

So your leadership team has gone out and made a concerted effort to listen, look, and learn. You have collated data, stretched your bladders with endless coffee and tea catchups with people, and worn out the soles of your favorite shoes by walking the halls, and you are now a premium customer with SurveyMonkey. It's time for your team to take stock of what you've learned and analyze it in a systematic, dispassionate way that will prepare you to take specific action.

USE ROOT CAUSE ANALYSIS TO TARGET YOUR CHALLENGES

We advise leaning on a trusty tool we use in most of our workshops around the world: *the root cause tree*. If you read our first book, *Edupreneur*, you will recognize this tool. For those of you who are new friends, we will step through it here, with a small but important difference. In *Edupreneur*, we helped teachers identify a specific problem, dig down to understand that problem, and then build a focused solution to make a change. As such, people used one root cause tree to step through one problem.

For you, though, a reader of *Dream Team* and someone on the Change Leader Journey, things step up a level. Your leadership team doesn't have just one problem that you are analyzing with one tree; you may have problems enough for an entire forest.

Once you learn the technique we're about to cover here, you are likely to use it to solve a whole bunch of challenges. For now, we recommend that you focus on the three most compelling challenges that you have identified through all your listening. These challenges—these problems—should be real, solvable, and—for an extra gold star—aligned to the passions of your team (as in, you are actually excited to solve them). Also make sure that at least one of your targeted challenges focuses explicitly on learning. This is, we know, often the biggest lever to pull for improved outcomes. If you haven't already identified your top three change priorities, pause your reading and, as a team, write this on a piece of paper: "The three problems we think we most want to solve are . . . ." Then complete the list.

All set? Excellent.

Eventually, you will step through the root cause analysis process for all three of the challenges your team has identified, but for now, as you learn the technique, choose just one of them. We say this knowing that the competitive folks and Type As will want to tackle all three in tandem. If that's your team, have a go at it!

A word of warning, though, before we get started: *Follow the process and don't jump ahead.* We do this training work with thousands of people every year and always see one or two in every workshop say, "Oh, I've got this!" and rush through on their own. When we lean over their shoulder and look at their work, we almost always have to break the sad news that "Sorry, no—you don't got this." If you're tempted to work ahead, just think about that time you tried to build a piece of IKEA furniture without reading the instructions. Yes, that's how it'll go. Step through this process with us.

To start, grab a piece of paper and draw a picture of a tree, something like the one in Figure 2.1. You want a thick trunk, some thick branches and roots, and then thinner branches and roots coming from them.

Figure 2.1

Root Cause Tree

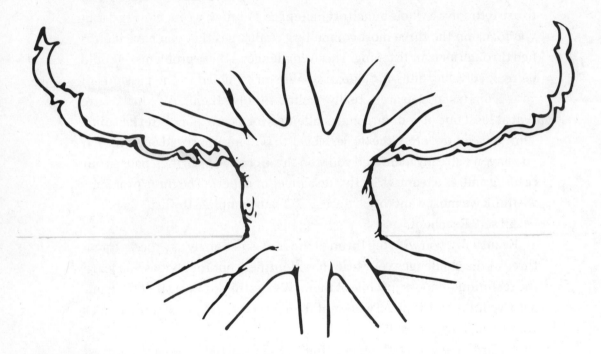

The trunk

In the trunk of your tree, write your challenge—one of the priority problems you are up against. Keep it really simple. Examples might be

- Kids aren't finding class time fun.
- Kids don't feel safe at school.
- Our team is not working well together.
- Parents are not engaged in the school's work.

For this tool, the more simply you state the problem, the better. We are going to step through an example—"Our team is not working well together"—with you now (see Figure 2.2). After you identify your problems, come back to your tree, fill in the trunk with one of them, and model your inquiry on what we do.

Figure 2.2

Root Cause Tree — The Trunk

The problem . . .
our team is not
working well
together.

The branches

In the branches of the tree, detail the *consequences* of the problem. What happens because this problem exists? The branch size reminds you to articulate these consequences specifically and precisely.

So if the challenge is that our team is not working well together, maybe we see its effects in poor community perception, stressed staff, poor communication, privatized practice, and reduced productivity. As Figure 2.3 shows, the most obvious consequences go in the big chunky branches.

Figure 2.3

Root Cause Tree—The Branches

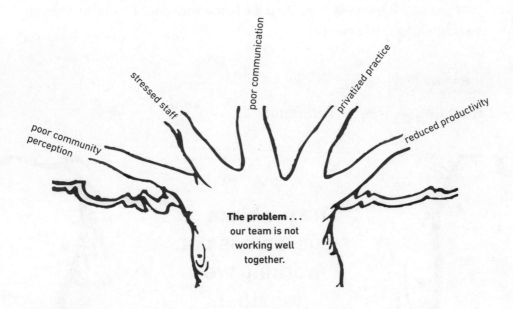

Once you have the major consequences down, add additional branches—smaller outgrowths—to explore each consequence. Check out, in Figure 2.4, how far we have extended the "Poor community perception" branch.

One reason to really spend time on this part of the tree is that the better you understand the problem and its consequences, the more you can stick up for the solution you offer and the more leverage you'll have to begin and sustain the necessary work. A thorough understanding of the consequences of your problem can help get your immediate team on board, but it is also a great tool that the team can then use to explain to both internal and external parties why you have chosen a particular challenge as your focus.

Figure 2.4

Root Cause Tree—The Extended Branches

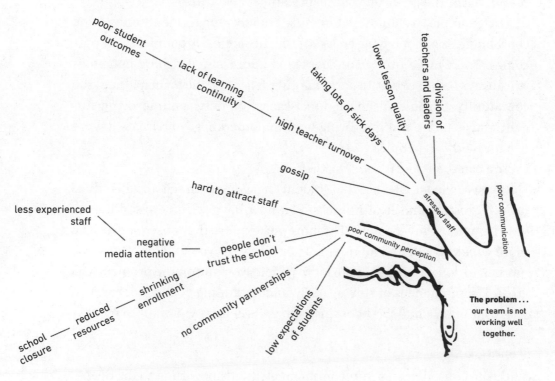

See, the reality is that as a leadership team, you will be under constant pressure to address a whole range of issues. The priorities you think you should be focusing on may be ever-changing, based on community pressure, political timing, or even the latest report from a university or think tank. If you are lucky, the focus of the day might align with the problem you are trying to solve . . . but best not to rely on luck.

Knowing the consequences that result from *not addressing your problem* is vitally important to the various players to whom you need to justify your strategic focus. If you can go deep into the consequences and show alignment and wins for them, you might be able to get some traction and resources for the problem your team wants to focus on.

For example, if you are addressing student engagement, one of the consequences of not having engaged students is clearly poor learning outcomes. You can be pretty confident that addressing learning outcomes will always be important to parents, other teachers, the principal, and the community. If you can show a direct causation between improving student engagement and improving learning outcomes, you create a win–win for plenty of people.

You can then take it a step further.

If you can make the case that student engagement in school will reduce juvenile justice and health issues, you now have wins across different departments of government. The more you explore the consequences, the more wins you will find for others. The more wins you find for others, the more help you will get. And the more people working on the problem, the greater your chances of solving it. By understanding your branches, you give your team a massive boost in making the change you want to see.

The roots

With the consequences of the problem clear, it's now time to dig deep—to explore the circumstances that brought that problem about. Yes, we're getting to the root cause analysis part of our root cause analysis tree. If "our team is not working well together," why might this be so? Maybe . . .

- We are all too busy.
- Our schedules don't match up.
- Staff don't get along.
- Planning together has not been fun before.
- We don't know one another's strengths.

As shown in Figure 2.5, root causes go on the tree's big roots.

Figure 2.5

Root Cause Tree—The Roots

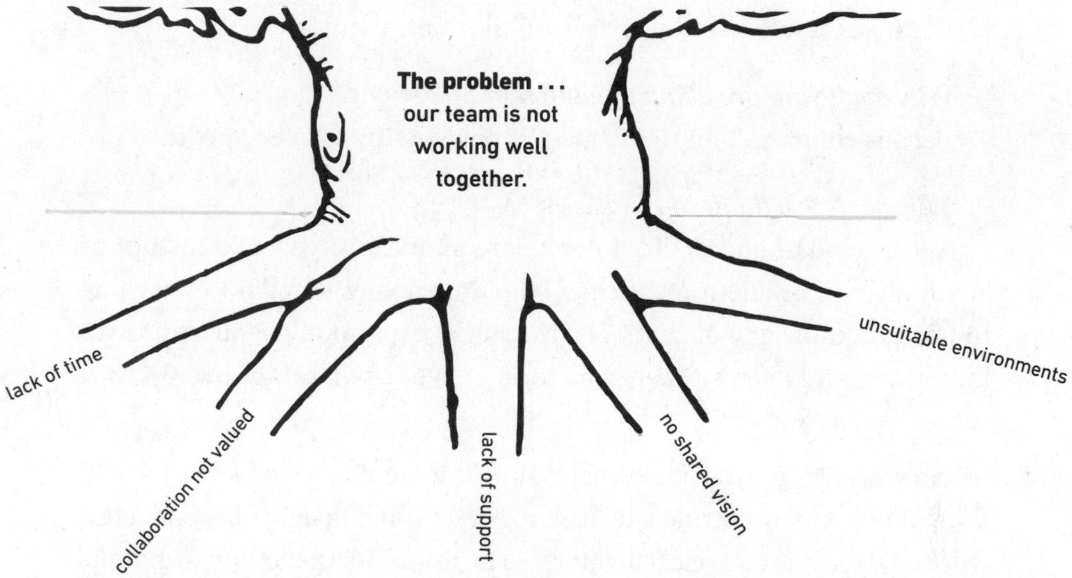

The problem . . .
our team is not
working well
together.

lack of time

collaboration not valued

lack of support

no shared vision

unsuitable environments

And now, as you did with the branches, go ahead and extend those roots by delving into what might be contributing to the various causes of your problem. The easiest way to do that is to focus on a single root at a time and start asking, "Why?"

Let's practice via an imaginary conversation with a student who finds school boring. In this example, we'll commit to five rounds of "Why?" (a.k.a. the 5 Why technique):

Why don't you like school?
Because it's boring.

Why is it boring?
Because the teachers talk about boring stuff.

Why do you think the things the teachers talk about are boring?
Because I don't care about the stuff they talk about.

Why don't you care about the stuff they talk about?
Because it doesn't matter to me. I'm never going to use any of it.

Why don't you think you will use it?
Because what good is it? I don't care about 200-year-old history or about algebra or about a bunch of stupid poems. When am I ever going to need to know any of that? The teachers keep talking about it like it's important, and I just sit there wondering, "When will this be over?"

Now we are getting somewhere. In this example, we have performed a small miracle by getting a teenager give us some insights beyond a few words. (Dave has teenage daughters, so he attempts the 5 Why technique quite often!) If we were to dig even deeper into this student's thoughts, we might trace them back to teaching that was straight from the textbook, or we may find that there is not a great deal of project-based learning happening in the school. Just from this exploration alone, it is clear that this student in particular can't see the links between classroom learning and the real world. That is a problem we can solve. Regardless of where the inquiry eventually takes us, we're bound to end up with better and more helpful information than "school is boring."

You can use this 5 Why technique to construct a pretty comprehensive root system. As the example in Figure 2.6 illustrates, there's no need to hold back, and it's fine to keep things casual. You're looking for interesting insights, not necessarily research-backed evidence.

Now, to set up the next step in root cause analysis, we are going to do what we love doing: tell a story. Well, Aaron's going to tell it.

Figure 2.6

Root Cause Tree—The Extended Roots

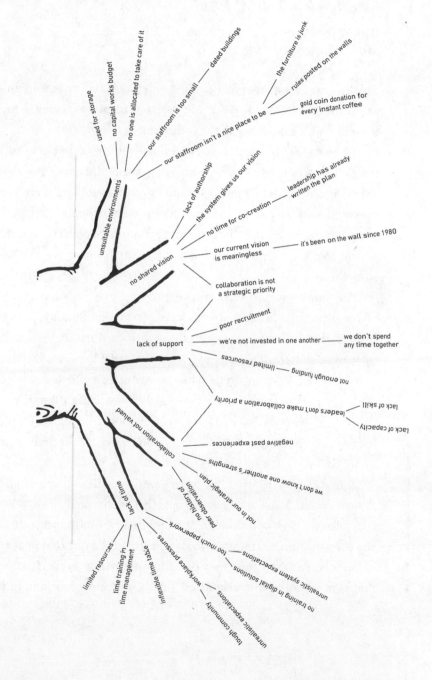

When Insights Save Lives

Aaron Tait

Makuyu, Kenya, 2009

Kaitlin and I spent the year leading an HIV/AIDS orphanage in the small village of Makuyu. Over that year, our team was trying to tackle a whole raft of challenges in the community.

We completed many root cause analysis trees, but one of the tougher ones was where we wrote in the trunk, *Girls are missing too many days of school*. The consequences of this problem were heartbreaking. Our female secondary students were dropping out, getting pregnant, contracting STIs, remaining trapped in poverty, and dying young. We knew these girls. They were our friends. We had to do something.

For months we listened, working to improve our understanding of the problem. We chatted with girls' parents on Sundays and with their teachers after school. We talked with the girls at the markets. We played soccer with their boyfriends and tried to gain some insight from half-time conversations. These investigative efforts revealed all sorts of root causes: the need for the girls to work their family's land, that there were few educated female role models, that many of the girls found school boring, and the feeling among parents that they couldn't afford to invest in the girls' education.

One day though, when we were chatting with a group of girls, I casually asked, "How many days a month do you usually miss?" When they blushed and said timidly, "Around five," I excused myself from the conversation, and Kaitlin took over. It turned out that girls were skipping class every time they had their menstrual cycle. This problem is now commonly recognized among educators working in very poor communities, but back then—even with the seven degrees our team members had among us—it was the first that we had heard of it. We went back to the massive root cause tree we had drawn on a wall with chalk, scanned the dozens and dozens of different roots at its base, added this new one, and circled it. We figured if we could address this issue—eliminate this one cause—we would take a big step closer to solving the problem of girls dropping out of school.

DECIDE WHICH ROOT CAUSE YOU'LL TARGET FIRST

Now it's time for you and your team to do what Aaron and his team did.

Look, we know you hate the *entire tree*. It's got a giant problem spray-painted on its trunk and enough horrible consequence-branches to block out the sun. We know how much you want this tree to die. (This is a metaphor. You don't want real trees to die!) But what usually happens is that leadership teams facing big challenges, desperate to get their school out of the shadows, hack away at their problem's various consequences (the branches) and never target the roots. This is almost always the wrong approach, because just like on a real tree, branches grow back, often even stronger than before.

So, as a team, take a look at all of the root causes of your problem. Then look past the ones you don't feel equipped to handle right now, those you don't think will have enough of an impact on the problem, and those that seem out of your control. And then put a big circle around the root that you are ready to take on as a leadership team, as we have done in Figure 2.7.

Rather than throw yourselves at that huge problem on the trunk, your team will target this one refined and well-understood root cause of that problem. And because this is advanced work you're tackling here in *Dream Team*, you'll also construct additional root cause analysis trees for your two *other* priority problems.

Figure 2.7

Root Cause Tree—The Circled Root

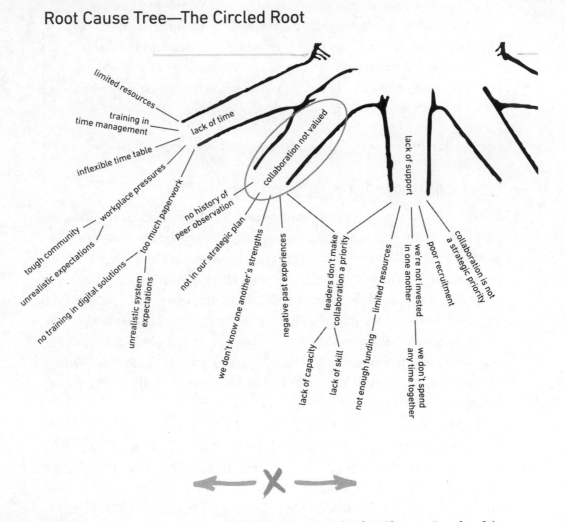

Having circled your root causes, the next step in the Change Leadership Journey is to figure out what to do about them.

3
FOCUS

How can we focus on a few specific areas for change?

At Lesher Middle School, there are Viking helmets everywhere.

Plastic helmets hang in the offices of leaders. They rest atop the desks of teachers in classrooms. Lesher's Viking helmet logo is on every newsletter and every poster. Students refer to themselves as either Vikings or Viqueens. Google the school, and the first result is their official website with the tagline "Welcome to the Ship." Perhaps more than any school the two of us have walked into before, Lesher has an identity.

That identity is wrapped around football posts and emblazoned on the indoor basketball court. Tall banners hang proudly from the top of the gym ceiling, proclaiming sporting achievements. To someone not used to a school like this (that includes us), at first glance, Lesher feels like the headquarters of a sports team. But dig just an inch beneath the surface and it's clear that the loyalty to the Lesher Vikings goes well beyond sports. In fact, the leadership team has drawn on the passion and loyalty people usually reserve for their favorite team and applied it to the pursuit of excellence. The rest of the community are signed up like season ticket holders.

Principal Tom Dodd and Assistant Principal Waren Morrow are so closely aligned on messaging that when interviewed, they sometimes give the same soundbites, word for word. And judging by Tom's recognition by the National Association of Secondary School Principals (NASSP) as the 2017 Principal of the Year, the messaging is working.

Ask individual members of the Lesher leadership team what the key mantras of the school are, and they can recite them verbatim. We repeatedly heard

- "High expectations, high support."
- "Everything happens in the context of relationships."
- "Content isn't king; caring is king."
- "We are an elite school, not an elitist school."

Beyond these regular mantras, the leadership team also come up with an annual message. For example, a few years back, it was "Row the boat," encouraging everyone in the school community to do their bit to support continuous improvement. This message was accompanied by the installation of a huge rowing oar at the front of the school and a year of professional development activity based on this message. The year of the "Anchor down!" mantra, climbing carabiners were handed out to members of the school community. Gold tokens are also pressed every year with key messages embossed onto them, and leaders give these out strategically as a source of inspiration.

what helps dream teams focus?

Lesher is a school that knows what it is about and lives this out, every hour of every day. What was interesting, however, is that when we asked the Lesher team what their school's vision, mission, and values were, the responses were not so consistent. In fact, lack of consensus on these three traditional business touchstones was something we saw at almost all the schools we spent time with for *Dream Team*. Instead, these schools all seemed to live by their particular mantras and focus areas. Here's a look at the ones we encountered:

John Polanyi Collegiate Institute

- "Students first."
- "Everything can be better."

John A. Leslie Public School

- "Our students are powerful users of ideas."
- "Our students challenge things and change them."

Challis Community Primary School

- "A positive and safe environment."
- "Teacher excellence."
- "A distributed and engaged leadership team."

Bayview Secondary College

These served less as mantras and more as key areas for strategic focus:

- "We will connect with community."
- "We will increase enrollment."
- "We will raise our academic profile."

Wooranna Park Primary School

- "Everything we do is to bring out the talent and passion of our students."
- "School should be as exciting as Disneyland."
- "Students are far more capable than we think."

Jeremiah E. Burke High School

We didn't note specific mantras at the Burke, but the focus areas there were both explicit and implicit:

- Support the whole child.
- Meet children where they are.
- Empathize with students' reality.

Chicago Tech Academy High School

The ChiTech team's collaboration with High Tech High meant project-based learning was a priority. They used the six A's structure created by Adria Steinberg (1997) to help them focus on the following areas:

- *Authenticity:* Does the project have meaning to the student, represent a real problem, and have real outcomes if solved?
- *Academic rigor:* Does the project apply to multiple content areas and foster higher-order thinking skills and habits?
- *Applied learning:* Does the project take place in real-world environments and foster real-world competencies?
- *Active exploration:* Does the project foster investigations and field-based work and result in real-world demonstrations?
- *Adult relationships:* Do students engage with adults as they explore the project?
- *Assessment:* Do students regularly and practically reflect on their learning with key criteria that are aligned with real-world standards?

Manurewa Intermediate School

The team's initial plan ("Countdown 75") was driven by the themes of *high visibility, communication*, and *interest in children*. These themes guided them to focus on

- *Kids:* Creating an engaging learning environment.
- *Staff:* Redefining a competent and passionate team.
- *Environment:* Rapidly creating a far more engaging learning space.
- *Community:* Uniting the community behind the change process.

When Countdown 75 transitioned into Rocketing 290, everyone's focus remained on those same four areas and adhered to the same three driving themes.

As you can see, these different schools all took different approaches. Some focused on overarching mantras, and others channeled their efforts based on a small number of key learning principles. But these mantras, themes, and principles all resulted from an approach called *simplexity*, the art of taking a complex thing and making it simple. Notice that none of these schools fell into the trap of having long, wishy-washy mission statements or visions. They didn't mention the oft-recycled and consultant-created values that we see in many other schools around the world, typically remixes of words like *respect, achievement, effort,* and *community*. (Apologies if any of these terms feature in your school's current set of values!) These words too often remain as just that—words. As we said earlier, a team-created line like "All of us are smarter than any one of us" is going to be more powerful than saying, "Remember everyone: *community!*"

What a leadership team needs at this step in the journey, when first considering how to tackle a root cause of a pressing problem, is not a perfect set of strategic priorities. You don't need perfectly crafted mission and vision statements. You just need a few short words that define what kind of change you're committing to bring about. These are the catch-cries that will help you focus—distinguish what matters most to you from everything else that also matters.

Also remember: you don't have the answers yet, and you haven't even started innovating your solutions. It's not about strategy right now; it's about focus. It's not about exactly what you'll do; it's about the direction you're committing to take.

setting your intention

In September of 1962, President John F. Kennedy gave a speech to a huge crowd at Rice Stadium in Texas. At the time, there was a strong feeling that the United States was losing the space race to Russia. Cosmonaut Yuri Gagarin had been successfully launched into space the year before, and NASA's Mercury Project had suffered a series of failures and setbacks. Public support of the U.S. space program was at an all-time low.

From the stage that day, President Kennedy publicly set a clear goal: "We choose to go to the moon in this decade."

It was bold statement. Audacious. And for many people in the audience, including many of the NASA scientists, it seemed unrealistic. People squirmed in their seats. They muttered doubtfully under their breath to one another. Yet as JFK continued speaking, he repeated this phrase three times: "It will be done." No room for confusion there. Despite the huge challenges ahead, the target was clear: a man on the moon, within eight years.

What's your team's moonshot? Your ambitious target? What will be the focus of your team's work? We have three simple strategies that can help you answer these questions.

REPHARASE YOUR ROOT CAUSES AS CORRECTIVE STATEMENTS

In Step 1 of the Change Leader Journey, you started by looking at the few key challenges that your team was inspired to unite around. Then, in Step 2, you listened to your community and used the insights they provided to flesh out root cause trees for each of these challenges and identify a single root cause of each to target. So the simple thing to do here, in Step 3, is to take a look at the three root causes that you circled on your three root cause trees and rephrase them as corrective statements of intention. For example, in our tree (see Figure 2.7), we circled *collaboration not valued*. So one of our focus areas would be "We are going to value collaboration in our school."

Other examples of corrective statements (from other root cause analyses) might be "We are going to care for the whole child, even before learning takes place" or "Our students will be prepared for the future, today."

REVISE NOW IF IT DOESN'T FEEL RIGHT

This is important. If your team is looking at these root causes and feeling like they are not the focuses that you want to go after, you need to take a step back. Look again, more closely, at your root cause tree. Review the data you gathered from your listening time. You might even go all the way back to Step 1 and consider if your team is still united around the same challenges.

MAKE YOUR FOCUS OFFICIAL

In the last chapter, we asked you to create three root cause trees, focused on three problems. Go ahead and turn these into the statements that will define the next chapter of change that your school is going to move into. Do try to limit yourself to three statements; as we often say, if you have more than three priorities, you have no priorities. Also, the shorter and punchier your statements, the better. "We choose to go to the moon in this decade" is a pretty amazing benchmark. Get these down on paper under the title "The Three Root Causes We Will Focus On." If you make your list on a whiteboard, take a photo of it.

With these key statements decided and recorded, you are now ready for the next step in the Change Leader Journey. It's about ensuring your new direction is aligned with what your system would like you to do, and about working for the autonomy you need to implement the solutions you devise.

4
ALIGNMENT AND AUTONOMY

*How can we gain the confidence
and authority we need to make the
change we want to see?*

Lindsa McIntyre had been the principal at Jeremiah E. Burke High School for only six months. She inherited a situation where only one-third of the school's students were graduating and there were more suspensions each year than there were students. She and her team were facing a huge challenge—one that they were just beginning to get their heads around.

And then Lindsa received a letter. We'll let her describe the moment:

> *The state identified us as a school that was struggling and in need of improvement. We were labeled as a "level four, underperforming turnaround school." When I first heard the language, I was hurt by it. I remember crying.*

Most change processes start with a moment like this. While not all of these moments involve news this dire, there is always a realization that something must be altered if a struggling school is going to survive or a successful school is going to remain successful. Nor does the timing of these moments always seem fair. Like Lindsa at the Burke, many school leaders feel some frustration that they are inheriting a set of challenges and administrative burdens that were not of their making. Some people deflect the blame; others assume responsibility. Lindsa is the latter kind of leader.

> Then, as I sat there with tears in my eyes, there was this awakening. I read on through the letter, realizing that this gave us huge opportunities. There was the opportunity to restaff the school, to redesign the school. There was the opportunity to engage a group of teachers, leaders, local stakeholders, and family members in a process of change.

The system stepped in and set Lindsa and the Burke some big goals. But how she would achieve these goals was up to her—and up to the leadership team that she would begin selecting.

Several states to the west of the Burke, the team at Chicago Tech Academy High School received a similar letter from the Board of Education.

The school had opened in 2009 as the passion project of a group of Chicagoans who had found great success in the tech industry. ChiTech's goals were simple: to provide a high quality of technology education in order to create opportunities in the tech sector for young people living in the city's South and West Sides. Essentially a charter school, ChiTech still requires a city license to operate and still uses city funding. Any shortfall in running costs is made up through fundraising and philanthropy.

Unfortunately, despite much hard work and high levels of passion from the founding team, ChiTech's education outcomes remained low—so low, in fact, that the city authorities announced the school had one year to turn things around or it would be shuttered.

It was in these troubled times that Linnea Garrett was hired as the new instructional leader. She was up to the challenge of rapidly improving

ChiTech's educational outcomes—looking forward to it, even. And that was because she had been given the autonomy to try new things. Here's Linnea:

> *The system administrators had basically told us that they would be back in six months to see what was happening. The school board and some key leaders were excited about exploring a partnership with deeper learning pioneers High Tech High in San Diego, but beyond that, the brief was that they trusted me to get things done.*

Like Lindsa in Boston, Linnea was given specific targets to hit but also the freedom she needed to figure out the means to those ends. For schools in such unfortunate situations overall, this was good fortune indeed.

all kinds of leaders can be change leaders

Our organization, Education Changemakers, strives for great outcomes that can scale to impact many. And in our past nonprofit work, we have helped bring about enormous benefits for hundreds of thousands of people living in poverty. Yet we are often frustrated when great ideas in education fail to disseminate beyond individual sites.

We were therefore validated by Michael Fullan's work on coherence and the points made in his and Joanne Quinn's book *Coherence: The Right Drivers in Action for Schools, Districts, and Systems* (2015). If you haven't read it, grab yourself a copy; it is good stuff. But for the sake of keeping you moving through *this* book, we'll summarize Fullan and Quinn's key points here.

They advocate that schools in a given system seek united approaches rather than engage in radical "outlier" activity, and their rationale is a clear and optimistic one. As they put it, "When large numbers of people have a deeply understood sense of what needs to be done, and see their part in achieving that purpose, coherence emerges, and powerful things happen" (p. 1). For those who might think "coherence with the system" implies more reporting requirements and more directives from the head office, Fullan and Quinn are quick to clarify: "Coherence is not structure. It is not alignment. It consists of the shared depth of understanding about the purpose and nature of the work" (p. 1).

When we started to identify leadership teams who had successfully brought about major change in their schools for this book, we discussed whether we should look for teams of radicals or ones that worked closely with the system to achieve change. We decided to put the question directly to the leadership teams we were meeting with: *Do you see yourselves as radicals, or are you darlings of the system?* The answers we got back were a mixed bag, which is a bit ironic, seeing as how we were looking for coherence. Go ahead and read these responses for yourself.

Challis Community Primary School

"Some would say we were pretty brave in the early years to do what we did, and we certainly pushed back often on what the system wanted us to do. But that didn't come from a desire to be radical; instead, it probably came from naiveté."

Manurewa Intermediate School

"The system was out of ideas. There was a sense [that] letting Iain Taylor and his team into the building [was a bold step] and a confidence that he could build a team to fix it. That autonomy was increased by the flexibility the system gave us as a school, led by our appointed trustees. We worked within the legal frameworks, but we were creative and able to demonstrate wins for the head office."

Bayview Secondary College

"To be honest, we kind of went alone to begin with. But then, as things started to work, we began to make noise and really engage with the system. We were too insular for too long, but we figured out how to show wins for the system and also how to tap into their support."

Lesher Middle School

"Absolutely we are radicals."

Then, from Lesher, an immediate clarification: *"But we have a great relationship with our school board. They give us freedom because we consistently demonstrate wins for them."*

John Polanyi Collegiate Institute

"The Toronto School Board superintendent assigned to our school gave us lots of autonomy to form our vision. It was inspiring to have that space. So we did things differently, but we also knew how to work with the system to assure them that things were happening. Creating positive relationships with people across the system was important to us."

John A. Leslie Public School

"We were radicals. Lots of people in Toronto were picking specific expectations from the system list and targeting them. To be honest, we saw a disjuncture from what the academic theory was telling us to focus on and what we were seeing in practice for our students. We leaned back from all this and asked, 'What is the big skill that we are really trying to foster in our kids?' Our answer to that was what we went after."

As the Lesher team had done, the leaders at John A. Leslie followed this with some tempering comments: *"We had some people in the leadership team who paid their ways through college as salespeople. So we knew how to frame what we were doing in a way that kept the system happy, and if we did this, given how big the system is, they pretty much left us alone."*

Cornish College

"We had a very different view to the system leaders at the main campus. There was a very powerful feeling that we could get this done and show them what was possible when people thought differently."

Jeremiah E. Burke High School

"We are radicals. And the turnaround conditions gave us the chance to be radicals, which was interesting. The district trusted leadership to make things happen, and we demonstrated wins, with hard numbers, quickly. In

fact, we are striving to get some of that autonomy back; ironically, we lost a lot of it when we were taken off turnaround status."

Chicago Tech Academy High School

"The feeling was that our students weren't motivated to learn, but that was wrong. A system always creates the results you set it up to. So if you want different results, you need a different system. We are radicals, and we usually ask for forgiveness rather than permission. But increasingly we are reaching out to others to share what we are doing and to learn from them about how we could be better."

Wooranna Park Primary School

"The school is lonely, and very few other schools would understand what we do. We think we need to change the system, not the child. We were a self-governing school in the early days, which gave us huge flexibility that we certainly made the most of. We don't have that anymore, and it is frustrating."

Wooranna Park is probably the one outlier on this point, a clear radical in their system, and more closely aligned with like schools around the world than with those in nearby suburbs. But their leadership team admits to a feeling of loneliness, which often goes hand in hand with renegade status.

The other schools and their leadership teams seemed to have straddled the line between coherence and independence. They had—or managed to carve out for themselves—a measure of self-determination, and this allowed them to try new things based on what they were seeing in their context.

This autonomy came in a few ways. Some Dream Teams inherited it as a governance structure, with the school earmarked as a self-governing school or led by an independent board of trustees (usually members of the local community). Others were granted autonomy as a last resort, after school boards had perhaps concluded that traditional approaches hadn't worked, so they might as well hire a strong leader and gamble that he or she could assemble a team and change things. Still other Dream

Teams chose to ask for forgiveness rather than permission—putting themselves at risk of doing the "wrong" thing in the system's eyes but operating on the belief that their ideas were informed by research, contextualized to the realities of the school, and led by a united and passionate team. Despite some reprimanding from the head office, they were usually successful.

balancing independence and coherence

After a long day of researching, we found ourselves sitting over a cold beer at the local, arguing about which superheroes we could see represented among the leadership teams that we spent time with for this book. The funny thing was, almost every one of them came out as Batman.

Batman does what he does to keep Gotham safe. He certainly has some radical ways of doing this, with an interesting choice of uniform, transport, and techniques, but almost always, he gets the job done. And while Batman is not a fully accepted member of the Gotham City Police Force, and sometimes they have to pull him into line, they usually like his work, shining the bat signal high into the sky when they need his help. Like Batman, most of the leaders of the Dream Teams in this book employed somewhat radical techniques but achieved enough wins for the system to allow them to keep operating. And don't forget, Batman doesn't really have superpowers; he relies on good R&D, well-selected tools, and trusty sidekicks like Robin and Alfred to help him out. Like Batman, changemakers strategically engage with the system to maintain their autonomy.

Here are some ways you can do that, too.

PAY ATTENTION TO WHAT THE SYSTEM ENCOURAGES

As noted, transformation efforts are often triggered by a notification from on high that a given school needs to change. The district or independent school board then typically hires a leader that they feel has a track record or the right stuff to lead this chapter in the school's journey.

If you are the leader hired for this role, start by digging into the goals that the system leaders have, and then determine whether your approaches are aligned. If you can successfully make the case that your ideas align from the get-go, you should advocate at this early stage for the autonomy you and your team are going to need to truly respond to your school's realities. If the people hiring you are not forthcoming in these meetings, then maybe you are not the right person for this particular job, or you are not in the right system.

Aiman Flahat and the team at John Polanyi felt like they had the freedom to innovate but also had the benefit of knowing that the Toronto School Board shared their investment in student engagement and high expectations. When the John Polanyi leaders engaged with their system leaders to investigate the system goals, they stressed how well aligned their own objectives were. With this in mind, don't be afraid to go as high up in the chain as you can to show alignment with system goals and win greater support. Dave made this a focus for his external communications when he was principal at a number of schools. He never had to go all the way to the prime minister, but he was more than ready to do so.

FIND THE RIGHT DATA AND SHARE THE NUMBERS

While numbers are not the be-all-and-end-all in educational change, they are useful to tell a quick and powerful story. Michael Fullan (Fullan & Quinn, 2015) refers to this as *internal and external accountability*, where leadership teams make the effort to assess their outcomes with great clarity and effectiveness, and then share the key metrics with the system stakeholders to foster coherence. We will talk more about using data to make your case later in the book, but for now, think about the numbers you want to track over the long term, benchmark where you are before your leadership team gets to work, and then watch those magic metrics closely, celebrating every improvement along the journey. The more often you can demonstrate outcomes that are aligned with the system's goals, the more likely the system is going to support your change efforts.

BE WILLING TO CHANGE YOUR LANGUAGE

Try to think of "the system" as something more than a loose concept that levies restrictions on you. It's actually a collection of professionals who have goals, passions, and interests. There is every chance that they have chosen to take your district or region down a certain path because they have been convinced by school visits, talks they have heard at conferences, books they have read, or experiences they had as school leaders that it's the right course.

When people have set ideas about something, it can be hard to convince them to move in a different direction. So analyze the language your district leaders are using in their speeches, meetings, and directives—and shift *your* language to align more closely. For example, if you want to push future-focused skills but they keep talking about entrepreneurial skills, suck up your ego a bit and use their words. You may be surprised by how much more open they'll be to supporting you!

FIGHT TO RETAIN YOUR AUTONOMY AS YOU IMPROVE

Unfortunately, a number of the Dream Teams experienced a reduction in autonomy directly proportional to their rates of success. Essentially, the better their school performed, the less control they were left with. This is something for system leaders to consider. If a school achieves great things, perhaps it's best to continue giving them freedom to create rather than forcing them to conform to a standard way of operating. As school leaders, keep this in mind and keep fighting for your autonomy as you show improvements.

To recap, as a leadership team you have now done the following:

1. Shared and reflected on your passions, ensuring you have some clear alignment among you, and confirming that you have adequate energy for the transformation effort.

2. Devoted time to listening to your school's staff members, students, and parents to ensure you have informed insight into stakeholder concerns and a comprehensive look at your operations and challenges.

3. Distilled your challenges to no more than three key areas that you are going to focus on.

4. Started to walk that tightrope between finding the autonomy you need to operate and ensuring that where you can, you are engaging with the system and fostering coherence.

Now that you have thought about what the system thinks of your plans, you need to get ready for the reactions of another group: your community.

5
COMMUNITY

*How can we best engage our
community in this change?*

The e-mail announcing the shutdown came as a surprise to many.

The school had been operating for decades as a satellite site of a prestigious private institution closer to the city. It was located on acres of pristine wilderness land; environmental sustainability was baked into the learning style; and the students, their parents, and a committed staff absolutely loved what the school was offering.

But the number-crunchers at the head office were not as happy.

Declining enrollments, high maintenance costs, and large expenses budgeted for future infrastructure projects were all pointing to some rather concerning financials. Quite simply, the larger sponsoring school couldn't make the business model work at the satellite site.

The message arrived in staff and parent inboxes at 4:30 p.m. on a Friday. The school would be closed within a few months, and students would need to decide whether to commute 25 miles to the main site each day or find an alternative.

What happened next was not what the main office had expected. By 6:30 p.m., 30 parents had gathered at a local bar. The initial conversations were defined by a sense of outrage, a feeling that the decision made wasn't fair. Yet quickly, the confident and well-educated group of parents, many of them business leaders, started to wonder if there wasn't another path forward. Maybe there was a way the school could stay open. As a few drinks flowed, so too did the ideas. Parents with marketing experience gave their input into new communications concepts, strategy consultants creatively proposed new business models, and financial brains hypothesized new flows and uses of money.

Soon they had some sketches on the back of napkins summarizing what might be done. But what they didn't have yet was an idea of whether the rest of the parents, students, and staff were interested in digging in to try to save their school. Could they really get the community to come together to make this happen? They set a meeting for the next night to share these ideas with some of the satellite site's key leaders, take a closer look at the finances, and explore their options.

The satellite school had a student body of just under 300; however, across the two meetings held within days of the closure e-mail, more than 600 people came out to express their opinions. It's fair to say that the officials who set up these meetings to detail the reasons the satellite school would be shut down and outline the process for doing so were unprepared for the negative reactions they got from parents and the frustrated community. Later that week, the parent team held a town hall to garner support for keeping the school alive; 800 people attended.

Toward the end of the meeting, the revolutionaries who had spent the previous days coming up with an alternative plan were granted a few minutes' time to speak. The message they delivered was simple: *We think there is another way to keep this school open.*

While a few proposals were put forward, the leading option, built on their common passions and priorities and the feedback gathered from other staff members and parents, was to open a new independent school on the existing site. The school would offer (1) a continuation of the existing learning approach, (2) cheaper fees, and (3) the addition of grades 11 and 12 to take students all the way through to graduation.

Following a short presentation, the rebel leadership team asked for a show of hands: everyone who was eager to keep the school alive and willing to rally behind the new plan. Hands shot into the air. The support was unanimous. Next, they asked for volunteers—members of the school community with specific skills needed to complement the skills already present on the fledgling team. Fifty people answered the call, gathering in a classroom after the town hall meeting to throw their time and talents into the mix.

There is little doubt that main office leaders had been trying hard. But it appeared that they had lost touch with their satellite site staff, parents, students, and community. Stakeholders were not responding to the plan they were offering and wanted something else. The school did shut down but was soon reborn in an adapted format, with a new leadership team and a new name: Cornish College.

community prep

We've reach the part of the change effort that, within the world of education, is often called "stakeholder management." In the business world, it's called "comms and marketing." In our Change Leader Journey model, we call this step "preparing the community for the change ahead," and by "the community," we mean students, staff, parents, and system leaders.

To use another common metaphor, this is the point in the journey when leadership teams think they know where the bus is going. They think they know who will be driving the bus. Now they just have to get the community to climb on board. And—not to frighten anyone unnecessarily—this is the riskiest part of the Change Leader Journey. As Machiavelli said in *The Prince,* "There is nothing more difficult to take in hand, more perilous to conduct, or more uncertain in its success, than to take the lead in the introduction of a new order of things."

To increase your chances of nailing this step and decrease your chances of screwing it up, we're going to go over the points to keep in mind.

MAKE THE URGENCY CLEAR AND COMPELLING

The reality is that many people don't like change. It is messy and confusing, and there are almost always a few staff members or parents who will take things personally or be upset by the suggested new order of things.

Change is hard.

And because change is hard, your team needs to convince the majority that the change is necessary and that the effort will be worth it.

The easiest place to start is by demonstrating that the status quo is not acceptable. Don't get personal here by blaming individuals. Instead, frame the current situation as the result of many decisions influenced by many different factors, including the fact that things change and schools should change with them.

There are certainly situations where the case is clear. Cornish College, for example, had a tight deadline linked to the shuttering of the school. The new leaders had days to propose an alternate direction—days, not months. In contrast, the leadership team at Bayview Secondary College had a lot more breathing room. They framed their case for change as, "We need to connect with our community far more effectively, increase our enrollments, and dramatically improve our academic profile. If we get this right, we stay alive and thrive. If we get this wrong, the future of the school as we know it is uncertain."

At Chicago Tech Academy High School, the situation was similar. The leadership team was able to say to the community, "The city has given us six months. If we don't turn things around by the six-month review, the lights won't turn on next year."

When Jeremiah E. Burke High School was formally placed in turnaround status, its leaders received clear written directions that they needed to change out 50 percent of the staff, bring in a new learning approach, and meet very specific improvement targets. Failure to do so would result in even more drastic oversight from the municipality.

At Lesher Middle School, the situation was less urgent but no less challenging. In a town where plenty of compelling educational options were only a short drive away, Lesher's lack of distinction was a problem. The school's enrollment had dropped, and its large physical campus, expensive to maintain, was located on increasingly valuable real estate. Unless Lesher could prove itself as a school, the land would be requisitioned for another purpose.

In many schools, the drama isn't so intense. The change effort isn't an imperative response to outside forces; it's kicked off when fresh eyes are able to diagnose an organization that is operating below its potential, and fresh voices are able to articulate how things could be better. Such was the case at John A. Leslie Public School. Over the decade preceding Greg McLeod's arrival, the demographics of the school's suburban Toronto neighborhood shifted from largely white to majority minority. Greg found himself at the helm of a school with a student body that was 63 percent Bangladeshi-Canadian, and many of the students and families had been in the country for less than five years. Although John A. Leslie's students had changed, the school had not.

Wooranna Park Primary School had developed a name as a gifted and talented satellite school, providing high-quality advanced learning opportunities for the best students via extra workshops. However, the rest of its students were offered a far more standard education experience. Ray Trotter assembled a team that thought Wooranna Park could do better for all its students. As they discovered, questioning the status quo in a school where some of the student body are thriving complicates the case for change. The proposed alternatives need to be very strong if you hope to win converts. This is often the challenge for leaders in well-resourced schools that are getting good academic results but are still largely traditional.

And then there are the schools that, prior to change efforts, just weren't very good and hadn't been good in a long time. For those communities, it's not so much that change is unthinkable but that it's not thought of at all.

That's how it was at Manurewa Intermediate School. Located in South Auckland, a part of the city with an associated stigma of crime and generational poverty, Manurewa had a long record of poor academic results. And nobody seemed to mind too much. Leadership teams seemed to get a pass, due to the common impression that Manurewa was a difficult place to work, and its students would always be tough to teach.

Challis Community Primary School was in a similar state. Many of the children who attended this school, located in a working-class suburb of Perth, came from single-parent households. Again, the challenging context had long excused leadership teams from accountability for poor results.

And finally, there was John Polanyi Collegiate Institute, born of a messy merger of two underwhelming schools and situated in one of Toronto's tougher neighborhoods. Underresourced financially, housed in a building that was falling apart, and lacking focused leadership, the school was performing poorly, and few expected it to be capable of greatness. Leadership teams who come into schools like this, where low expectations are the norm, must demonstrate a great deal of courage, fresh ideas, and a touch of naiveté to sell an ambitious new future to a tired and skeptical community.

In all of these situations, making a case for change requires very clear communications, cut-through images and data, and a willingness to face facts. People need to be convinced that the status quo is no longer acceptable.

Think for a moment about that late-December, end-of-the-year feeling. If you are in the Northern Hemisphere, you are halfway through the coldest part of the year. You haven't been exercising much, but you've certainly been eating and drinking a lot—riding the tail end of celebrations that started with Halloween treats and continued through Thanksgiving, holiday happy hours, and cookie exchanges. The data sets are your bathroom scale display, that extra notch on your belt that you needed to shift to, and the pervasive feeling of bloat. The sometimes-shocking images and story are what you see in the mirror. And together, they convince you it's time for change: the gym, more vegetables, better sleep, and so on. What leadership teams assembling a compelling case for change need is something that will engender a similar sense of resolve. That something is clear data.

Identify the most definitive data sets that you can to show that a problem exists, and then present them with clarity and simplicity. To be blunt, the greater the slopes on your graphs, either up or down, the more compelling your data will be. Before and after images of a degraded school are also powerful—symbolic representations of the absence of pride or engagement that must be remedied. These stories don't need to be *The Lord of the Rings*–style epics. The shorter and more to the point you can be with your community, the better.

THINK ABOUT WHO IS HOLDING THE MICROPHONE

We find it interesting that at least half of the principals we spent time with for this book described themselves as reluctant speakers, shy even. They told us that when they could, they deferred the role of public speaker to a charismatic deputy or assistant principal, or they brought in different speakers for single presentations, asking them to play different roles. Public presentations are an essential tool for getting a community to accept a new direction. Be intentional about them.

If it is likely, or even possible, that the presentation's topic will be controversial, then the most senior leader should be the one holding the mic. The buck stops with the senior leader, and he or she needs to take full responsibility for the decisions being made. This is not to say that other members of the leadership team can't present different parts of the story, though. In a few pages, we'll dig into the details of this kind of communication and go over what to say and how to say it.

TALK MORE ABOUT THE FUTURE THAN THE PAST

There's a saying that's brought up often in schools: "Every adult thinks they know how school should run because they went to one themselves." When you are trying to bring about change as a leadership team, you'll almost certainly see this adage come to life. People (parents, in particular) can sometimes fall into factions and present and defend opinions informed by the latest book they read, the latest documentary they watched, or something they saw online.

When introducing change to your school community, it's important to communicate the reasons behind it and that it's not just change for the sake of change. Then, without painting too dystopian a future, invest some time highlighting the challenges you'll need to face together. Acknowledge the things the community might be worried about and assure people that the changes you propose are not about throwing the baby out with the bathwater. Explain what you'll be holding steady (e.g., the proven basics of solid instruction) and share the data that you'll use to drive the school's new initiatives.

One school that we worked with introduced a new way of engaging with parents called 21CP (21st Century Parenting). It involved monthly meetings with parents, complete with snacks and drinks. Each meeting featured a guest speaker from a major company, tech startup, or interesting profession, and the speakers shared their insights about what the future might hold and how the school could better prepare young people to thrive in that future. The leadership team was able to win over stakeholders not by attacking the status quo but by helping their community get excited about what change could bring.

moving the elephant

The book *Switch*, by Chip and Dan Heath (2010), is full of great stories of change, but the big takeaway for us was their analogy of the elephant and the rider. Paraphrasing, the elephant—that big, heavy, hard-to-stop gray mass of an animal—represents people's emotions. On top of the elephant sits a tiny rider whose task is to steer the unwieldy and unwilling elephant in a certain direction. The rider is the logic.

The Heath brothers encourage change leaders to focus first on directing the rider, which means ensuring that there is a set destination and that some of the initial moves have been scripted. (This is the work of Steps 1–4 of the Change Leader Journey.) Next, say the Heaths, change leaders need to move the elephant—figure out how to coax it along the chosen path. So the elephant is people, your community. Moving them means focusing on motivation, tapping into the feelings of the community, providing inspiration, and building their enthusiasm for being part of the change.

Here are some approaches to try.

USE STORYTELLING

We think one of the easiest ways to move the elephant is through storytelling. As the Nigerian poet and author Ben Okri wrote, "Stories can conquer fear, you know. They can make the heart bigger."

Barack Obama was a master of this kind of storytelling, and his speeches during the 2008 U.S. presidential campaign offer tons of illustrations. In his acceptance speech on election night, he spoke about change—the momentous change represented by an African American rising to the office of president of the United States. Rather than leaning on his constitutional law training from Harvard, he told the story of 106-year-old voter Anne Nixon Cooper and the history that she had lived through prior to that day. If you want to see what storytelling can do, watch the video of that speech, which is readily available online.

So, with your community, tell the story of a school alumnus who has gone on to do great things. Talk about a student and teacher who worked together to dramatically improve that student's learning. Share about the last major change effort and how far the school progressed during that thrilling time. There is a basic rule of thumb when you are trying to communicate for change: *If you can give people goosebumps or make them cry, you've done well.*

USE VISUAL REPRESENTATION

People can also be moved by very clear representations of a situation. In *The Heart of Change*, John Kotter and Dan Cohen (2012) share a story about a large manufacturing company that was trying to reduce costs. To bolster support for saving money, an insightful executive presented his colleagues with a visual tableau: a conference table piled high with the 424 almost identical types of gloves the company was currently purchasing, with the price tags (ranging from $5 to $17) still attached. The display became a traveling roadshow, and it successfully shifted opinions in the company on purchasing processes.

If a pile of gloves can have that kind of impact, we educators are ahead of the game. After all, when children are involved or affected, appealing to people's emotions is a much easier task. Maybe make a visual display of a pile of library books that have not been borrowed once in the last year. Conduct a live demonstration in which students volunteer to respond to a rapid-fire set of questions they were all able to answer on the exam six months before but will likely struggle to remember now. Begin a meeting by asking students what they want to do for a job when they leave school (or asking parents what they would like their children to do) and then check in midway through the meeting by projecting statistics on the likelihood that artificial intelligence will make the named jobs obsolete within a decade. Consider your team's goals, your school's circumstances, and your students, and then put your imagination into it.

FOCUS ON PEOPLE'S PASSIONS

Getting directly to what people are most passionate about is another way to connect to their emotions and then boost their engagement. Frankly, if you're speaking to an audience of parents, this means talking about the safety, support, learning, and future of their children. If you're talking to teachers, it means tapping into their feelings about their profession, the powerful sense of purpose they feel as the shapers of children's lives.

Maybe your leadership team is very enthusiastic about data—many are, and it's a good way to be. Data sets are a powerful tool for logical persuasion. But see if you can't park that inclination for a moment and expand your toolkit by thinking of ways you might move people. Rather than presenting a folder with countless pages of spreadsheets, graphs, and words at every occasion, try appealing to people's hearts. It can do a lot to move the elephant and prepare your community for the sometimes-tumultuous years ahead.

BEWARE OF THE BLOCKERS

Every leadership team will encounter "blockers"—people who stand up to challenge your changes and argue against the direction you've set for the school. We have met plenty of them over the years, and all the teams we profiled for this book have come up against their fair share as well. In the face of this inevitability, we advise remembering the words of Jon Kabat-Zinnwe, founder of the Stress Reduction Clinic at the University of Massachusetts Medical School: "You can't stop the waves, but you can learn to surf."

Over the next few pages, we'll introduce you to the types of blockers we have met; you may have met them too. We'll share with you the most effective techniques we have found for getting them on board, or at least reducing their blocking effectiveness. (Note, please, that the "characters" we discuss in this section can be both male and female; the gender choices here are just us going for the cheapest puns.) If the blockers to change in your school are particularly resilient, you might also consult *Lead Me, I Dare You!,* an extremely handy book by Sheryl Bergmann and Judith Allen Brough (2007).

Al Ready

You and other members of your leadership team have just presented the identified challenges, spoken about the direction you'd like to set for the school, and explained your higher expectations. You wrapped up with a tear-jerking story. Now Al raises his hand and says something to the effect of "We already tried that," or "We attempted to do that five years ago and got nowhere." He is suffering from an easily diagnosable case of change fatigue—a condition that's very common in a profession that seems subjected to a constant swirl of "new and improved" processes, systems, strategies, and curricula. Maybe Al got burned by a failed change effort years ago, or maybe he has simply burned out over time.

So convince him it's going to be different this time.

When pitching Al on the change, portray a future that is both more appealing and more realistic. Do what you can to bring him into the process now and get his insights on what didn't work five years back. When your leadership team moves into the ideation phase (see Chapter 7), Al's information may help you create more effective solutions. And know that Al is going to need continual updates to keep him convinced that it truly is different this time. Managing this blocker is not a one-meeting move; it's an ongoing effort.

Mona Lisa and Charity Case

For Mona, everything is hard, and a lot of it is unfair. Just ask her, and she'll tell you. She has more report comments than anyone else and a crazy teaching load. She seems to have been assigned all of the most disruptive kids. (Don't feel bad if you're feeling a pang of recognition here; as teachers, most of us have been Mona Lisa at some point. The work we do is tough.)

Mona's pal Charity has a seemingly catastrophic life outside school: tumultuous personal problems, health issues, and constant setbacks that overshadow work. It's given her a strongly pessimistic worldview.

Mona Lisa and Charity Case, two bundles of joy, seem to be drawn together by a magnetic force. No enthusiasm can survive their combined powers, and they can destroy a meeting in seconds. Just as you are reaching the climax of presenting the new direction the school is going in, they interrupt with a zinger that takes the moment away from you. They also publicly run down your ideas, complaining that your talk of "high expectations" and people "taking control" just isn't realistic for them and dragging a few people down to join them in the abyss of negativity.

Both Mona and Charity want the same thing: attention.

So give it to them.

Shower them with acknowledgment. Highlight how hard they are working. Shine a light (where appropriate) on the difficulties they have overcome. Make it clear to everyone that Mona and Charity are valued members of the team, and that you are going to need them if the project is going to succeed. If you do this well, you might just have great additions to your crew.

May Belater

May quite likes the school. She has a nice job, and she quietly gets her work done and collects her paycheck. Change is a scary proposition for her, though, and she doesn't like things to be disrupted suddenly or for surprises to be thrown her way. When May hears about the new change initiative, she will immediately angle to shift the start dates further away. "The first semester is always so busy," she'll say, "and then it's exam time, and that's not a good time to start projects. Then it's the holidays, and you know how kids are slow to start up in the new year. Then it's testing, and by then, it's almost summer!" Maybe it'd be better to hold off until next year, May will suggest, before pausing and pointing out that next year is when the lower primary classrooms are scheduled to be painted, which will be very disruptive. Yes, there is always an excuse to push the project back. If May gets her way, nothing will ever happen.

So get your way instead.

May needs strict and immovable deadlines. Tell her the very clear and very confirmed dates that the leadership team has set for the change initiative and will stick to. Even better, give her an in-progress schedule, where a third of the dates have already passed and thus a third of the tasks have already been completed. You want May to see the momentum—that this is happening now, and it's not going to stop. If you are not already using an online project management tool like Trello (or one of the similar products available for free), start. It will make tracking the work and sharing the deadlines easier. And if May Belater happens to be a member of your leadership team, make sure she is not the one quarterbacking the project and tasked with hustling the team to hit deadlines.

Con Ceited

Con is good at his job. Very good. Just ask him. He happens to believe he is the best teacher in the school, a Clark Kent with extraordinary abilities hiding among the regular workers. No doubt his mother is very proud of him and has told him this his entire life. When your leadership team starts to present new ideas, Con is quick to point out that he won't be needing this new approach—*his* students are doing just fine.

Sometimes, the frustrating thing with Con is that he actually *is* good. The kids like him, and the parents do too. Although he might get good results as an educator, Con is not so good at playing with others. Your leadership team needs talent like Con, but you need him on the bus, not telling everyone that he is going to drive his own motorbike.

So tap into his ego.

Look for the most challenging task you have and bring it to Con. Tell him that if there's one person who can get it done, it's him. Invite him to become skilled in the new approaches so that his classes can be demonstrations for his colleagues. Maybe appoint him "director of collaboration" and see if you can redirect his focus away from his individual excellence. Show him how much more fulfilling organizational excellence can be.

Chip Shoulder

Chip loves the school. He loves the kids. He even loves most of the staff.

But he just really doesn't like the leadership team, or perhaps it's just one or two people on the leadership team he doesn't like. So Chip is not getting behind this new direction. Maybe somehow, somewhere, at some point, someone on the leadership team offended Chip in a significant way, and it's developed into a long-standing grudge. Whatever the origin, the conflict is real, and it is deep-seated. Chip is spoiling for a fight.

So challenge him.

Sometimes all it takes is a conversation between two adults, with an honest engagement on what it was that caused the upset followed by a generous offering of apologies, even if those apologies aren't reciprocated. But if this doesn't work, there is another easy approach. Find out who the disliked member of the leadership team is, and then minimize the amount of time that person has to hold the microphone and serve as the public face of the change. Or at the very least, minimize the time Chip and his nemesis must work together on change-related activities.

Lee Derr

Lee is a very accomplished leader, at least in his eyes.

He has read many best-selling leadership books and has held leadership positions his whole life. In fact, he might have held one at your school. He might even have filled a senior role for a period in an acting capacity. For some reason, though, he hasn't been selected for your school's leadership team. And this has cut him deep.

The trouble with Lee is that if his ideas are not going to be followed, he is going to make it harder for your leadership team. He will be thinking that he could be doing it better, and he may even state this publicly, undermining your efforts to transform the school.

So enlist him as an ally.

There is a powerful way to get Lee on board that we have seen in action (and often used ourselves). You may need to bite your tongue so hard that it bleeds to do this, but trust us, it works: invite Lee to mentor one of the more junior members of your leadership team. Ask if he'd be willing to devote 15 minutes of his time once a month for members of your team to bounce a few ideas off him and get his insights.

These could be the worst moments of some team members' month, or they could be great. In our experience, it often goes well for a few reasons. First, with all the reading Lee's done, and given his own experiences leading, he may have some good insights. Sometimes leadership teams can suffer from groupthink, and Lee can be a handy devil's advocate to help you see things from a different angle. Second, if Lee is mentoring some members of your team, suddenly he won't be interested in undermining what they are trying to achieve. No one wants to see their mentees fail, so Lee may even start rooting for some of you. And if he walks around claiming that some of the leadership team's ideas were actually his, or he advised on the new approach, you know what? Let him do it. It is amazing what can be achieved when you don't care who gets the credit.

Harry Up

For a while, it's impossible to see Harry as anything but an asset—a powerful and important member of the staff community. In fact, he may even be on your leadership team. Harry's the guy who is up-to-date on the developments in the profession. He is on Twitter and is connected with educators across the world, sending tweets late into the night. He loves education and gets very excited by the latest things that are coming online.

Harry will watch Sugata Mitra's TED Talk on the weekend and come in on Monday trying to convince everyone in the staff room that they should be putting computers in their walls. He spent Sunday afternoon doing that in his room, in case anyone wants to pop by. He'll have already created a hashtag (#computersinthewall) and be planning a new blog on the topic. He's just waiting for domain name approval before it is launched.

But then, another weekend will come, and Harry will watch a *60 Minutes* special report about the Green School in Bali. By Monday, he's head over heels in love with the concept. The computers in the wall gather dust while Harry's students sit under trees and learn about the mating cycles of a rare West African frog. And another month will pass, and Harry's eager to have five minutes in the whole-school meeting to present a great idea about eliminating grade levels, or starting every class with five minutes of meditation, or repainting all the classrooms orange—a color that fosters creativity.

You get the picture.

Are you thinking about someone on your team right now?

You might even be smiling.

People like Harry are awesome, and their energy to do great things for their students is infectious. At this point in the journey, though, they are a danger to the number one thing you are fighting for: *focus*. Right now, your goal is to present your focus areas to the school community in a way that will support everything that comes after. When everyone's collective attention should be concentrated on the targeted areas, the easily distractible Harry is bringing distraction.

So treat him like an elite race horse: put the blinkers on him . . . and a harness too, so that his speed and excitement can be directed to the right areas.

Set tasks for Harry related to your focus areas. If one of them is bringing deeper learning into your curriculum, for example, ask him to tap into his Twitter universe and get as much information as possible. Invite him to innovate loads of solutions, focused on authentic and real-world learning pedagogy. If he gets distracted, rein him back in, give him a high-five (now he is a human again, not a horse), refocus him where you need him, and repeat as necessary.

Lucy Lips

And last of all, there's Lucy. She is probably a charismatic member of your team and well-liked by many. She may be the last to leave Friday drinks and the friendliest person in the staff room. But whatever Lucy picks up as a team member or learns as confidante . . . Lucy shares. Before long, the snippets of information Lucy parcels out with a "Guess what I just heard?" and a "Don't tell anyone, but . . ." have morphed into rumors that can derail your team's change effort before it even gets started.

During World War II, the British government acknowledged how damaging rumors were when they put out propaganda posters with the simple message "Loose lips sink ships." An even more shocking poster shows a sailor drowning and the words "Someone talked." Powerful stuff, and a clear message: spread rumors and we will lose this fight. The same goes for your team's transformation effort. "Harmless gossips" can be anything but harmless.

Lucy thrives in the dark, as the one in the know.

So turn on the lights.

The way to deal with gossips is create a more transparent environment overall. Share all that you can whenever you can. As a leadership team, if you are hearing rumors, address them publicly. In the schools Dave led, he set up a whiteboard in the staff room with "Rumors you have heard this week" printed at the top. Staff wrote up the rumors anonymously, and leadership addressed them on a weekly basis.

There's our cast of change-blocking characters. Take a minute and think about who they are in your school, and consider coming together with your leadership team to discuss the blockers you have and how to get them to go where the school is heading.

how much to say, and to whom?

Does everyone need to know everything? Do they need to know it all right now? Leadership teams tend to worry that telling every single stakeholder what they have in mind for change can backfire and throw all their plans into disarray. It can, so here is some advice to consider.

BE THOUGHTFUL ABOUT GETTING THE INITIAL MESSAGE OUT

One of the takeaways from Cornish College's origin story is that presenting a new direction by e-mail is not a great move. Treat this step of the journey with the same gravity as a wedding proposal. Would you propose to someone by text message? Or e-mail? You probably wouldn't even do it over the phone. No, you would propose in person, most likely with a well-thought-out plan of what to say. You'd choose the setting carefully. Maybe you would have spoken with your future in-laws—your partner's parents—to get them on board with the idea. If you're a traditionalist, you might have a diamond ring to present, evidence of your commitment and a bit of sweetener to convince your beloved that accepting your offer is a great idea. You get down on one knee and hope for a yes.

Kneeling is not recommended when it's time to announce your school's new direction, but we do suggest you release the information to the right members of your school community, at the right time, in the right manner. Noting that you have already worked for your alignment and autonomy with district leaders in Chapter 4, the rule of thumb for the best order for this roll-out is to speak first to the core leaders in the school (beyond your leadership team), then to staff, then to parents, and then to kids. Depending on how the dynamic works in your school, you may want to shuffle this up. Indeed, some of the leadership teams we spent time with would start change announcements with the kids. You should be strategic about *when* you announce your new direction to the various stakeholders as well; for example a major announcement to senior students as they are taking exams could be highly distracting. Equally, if one group finds out that everyone else has known about a planned change long before you share the news with them, you could damage trust.

Consider working quietly to get a few key influencers in the school to see the merits of the new approaches before you make an announcement to the wider body; this way, when you go public, you will have allies who will be raising their hands and voices in support. This approach is reminiscent of how people who are crowdfunding for a new idea will ask friends to purchase products in the campaign's first 24 hours. It's a way to give the idea more credibility.

Once you work out your plan for who needs to know and when they should know, move quickly to execute it.

BE CLEAR THAT THIS IS A JOURNEY

You are still at the early stages of the Change Leader Journey, and it is important that, as a team, you clarify to your community that there is a lot of work to do. Make it clear that the challenges you'll be facing mean great opportunities. There are many ideas still to develop, and the change effort is likely to span years, not months.

An optimistic community is a great asset here, but not everyone is lucky enough to have one of these. So we recommend your leadership team fortify people for the journey ahead by highlighting all the great work that you have already done as part of this change process: your discussions of passions and priorities, the listening you've done, the analysis you've undertaken. Sharing this information and documenting your progress can make the change effort feel more real and more achievable to those who are newer to it.

Please understand, though, that full community buy-in always takes time. Not everyone will be with you immediately, and this is fine. Some people will need to slowly adapt to the new way of doing things. If you want to prepare yourself to play the long game, consider the model set by Ray Trotter and the leadership team at Wooranna Park Primary School. When we spoke with Ray for this book, he had been at the school 30 years. Ray grinned when thinking back to the early days, when they moved from a gifted and talented focus for the top 15 percent of students to a whole-school engagement strategy. "Some people were on board [from the outset]," he acknowledged, "but you must take your *whole staff* along with you, and that took eight years for us." The road can be long. Know that and prepare for it.

TAKE NOTE OF OTHER COMMUNITY RESOURCES

All of the leadership teams that we spent time with brought in significant support from outside the school. These included local and international nonprofit organizations, which provided funding and expert support, as well as powerful thinkers, who brought notoriety and credibility to the change efforts. They engaged with other schools, partnering to share resources and offer peer-learning across sites.

When asked about the power of partnerships, the leadership team at the Burke were able to point to more than 60 foundations, nonprofits, companies, and universities that they have worked with over the past five years. In their view, these partnerships were a core driver of their success. Similarly, the Wooranna Park team presented us with a piece of paper listing all of the groups and individuals who, over the years, lent influence and provided in-time support.

When you present your new direction to your community, don't be so focused on explaining your ideas that you overlook who is in the room and how they might contribute. Parents, staff members, community members, and students aren't passive information receptors; they're human beings. Some of them may be skeptics or even blockers, but they're also allies in waiting. What skill sets, resources, and connections do they have that might accelerate the change effort?

At Cornish College, for example, the leadership team that initiated the school's rebirth was bolstered significantly by parents, who contributed highly relevant and valuable skills for the change effort. The leadership team even received a financial donation from a set of grandparents who were so impressed with what was happening that they were willing to dig deep to help make this change a reality. We won't give away the figure, but we will say the donation was *not* small.

When you engage your community members as key players in the transformation, the resources they contribute can make the leadership team's work easier. If you're very lucky, you may even find you've got grandparents or some other champions with surprisingly deep pockets.

specific tips for "the talk"

So far, your leadership team has thought about who needs to receive your message, when it will be delivered, and who will be delivering it. You have focused on setting high expectations, preparing people for the journey ahead, and pushing through the change fatigue in a refreshing new way. You have even diagnosed some of the potential blockers and begun your efforts to get them on board.

At some point, you'll need to bring all the people in your community together and formally present the direction that you are hoping to move toward as a leadership team, a school, and a community. This is "The Talk."

At this point in the journey, you are not pitching your solutions (because you haven't even created them yet). You are simply explaining the challenges that you think exist, signaling your desire as leaders to solve them, and inviting your community to either be part of the process or just give you the thumbs-up you need to move forward.

When you bring a group of people together, how do you increase your chances of being warmly received? What should your leadership team say, and how should you say it?

We're going to present some tips for structuring The Talk—bearing in mind that many people do not enjoy public speaking, particularly when in front of a big audience at a potentially controversial meeting like this. It's a very good idea to review this section as a team and go through the points one by one. Yes, it will help your chosen speakers ace this all-important meeting, but it will also improve your presentation skills overall and help you come across with greater power when you talk with your community.

START WITH A STORY

In your talk, you have a matter of seconds to get people's attention and move them. So tell a story about the school, or a child, or a staff member. Stories are easy to tell, people like hearing them, and they change the dynamic immediately.

What you shouldn't begin with is your name, your role, where you sit in the organizational structure, a big long thank-you to everyone for coming tonight, and the locations of the exits and the toilets. And don't start the meeting with regular business and then squeeze in the change effort at the end. Make the entire meeting about it. Grab people's attention fast and give them something to lean into and get excited about.

USE YOUR NUMBERS

From the moment you start talking, some people will begin to doubt the direction that your leadership team is taking the school in. This is where you can use powerful numbers and interesting statistics to enhance the credibility of your ideas and make the case for change. The secret here, though, is simplicity and clarity. At this point in the journey, people don't want to hear from accountants; they want to be moved by leaders!

As an example, when Dave was working to convince his community that big changes were needed at Halls Creek District School, he pointed to one frightening number, impossible to brush off: on the day he started as principal, there were 300 students on the roll, and only 37 of them were present. As another example, we once watched a team of leaders presenting to parents their new approach on well-being and student support. The number they courageously shared was that at least half of the parents in the room had children who reported via an anonymous survey that they had experienced anxiety and depression in the past year.

To demonstrate the amount of listening you did, share some numbers and insight about that work: how many hours were devoted to this task, how many conversations you had, how many survey responses you received. Share examples of posters, newsletter articles, and social media posts where you encouraged community input. When the numbers hit close to home, people are more willing to move in the direction that leadership team is hoping to take the school.

HAVE A COUPLE OF KEY POINTS AND STICK TO THEM

Politicians and corporate leaders train for years to hone their messaging, but there is one thing your leadership team can do to make sure your main idea gets across. Before The Talk, take a moment to remind one another other of the key points that you decided to focus on at Step 3 of the Change Leader Journey (see p. 63). Write these down again somewhere, and if you need to, have them on stage with you. Then, throughout your presentation, repeat them constantly, ensuring that they are clear to all listening and that everyone will walk away knowing exactly what your team is aiming to do.

One school leadership team we worked with focused on improving the diets and overall health of their students through a combination of changing the menu in the school cafeteria and encouraging parents to send the children to school with wholesome food. Their key soundbite was "In a recent study, our suburb was found to be the most overweight in the state." They wanted to break this statistic and wanted the school to be a leader in the community on this issue.

A great way to check if your key points are coming across clearly is to practice your presentation with someone, and at the end, ask them: if they were to compose one tweet about it, what would they write?

INTERACT WITH THE AUDIENCE

Don't feel like your team needs to make a big long speech, throwing ideas at people for an hour. In fact, it's best not to do that!

Early in your talk, after you introduce your key points and share data, consider turning up some music to change the dynamic and asking audience members to turn to the person next to them for a quick discussion of what's been said so far. Instrumental jazz is a good choice, we have found, but you should choose music your community might like.

Earlier, we mentioned 21CP, the program created by a group of school leaders who were hoping to get parents to embrace future-focused learning. They knew their information evenings would draw a well-educated and highly engaged parent group, so they provided wine and cheese, and took time early in their first meeting to ask, "If you could teach your children one skill to thrive in the future, what would it be?" With this early interaction, the parents felt immediately engaged and more valued throughout the rest of the meeting. The school leaders were then able to weave in the audience's ideas with their professional and research-based approaches.

Interacting like this is risky, because you may have a few know-it-alls in the room, but we think it is worth the gamble, particularly if you can walk the fine line between getting a key message across and being adaptable enough to tweak this message as you engage with your community.

MAKE YOUR VISUAL AIDS ENGAGING

The most efficient way to convince your community that the "exciting new change" you are proposing is actually mutton dressed up as lamb is by explaining it via a boring old PowerPoint presentation. If you *do* choose to use slides during The Talk, we encourage you to spend a little bit of time making them look really great.

When creating slides, a great rule of thumb is the 10/20/30 rule from the Silicon Valley communications guru Guy Kawasaki (2005): never have more than 10 slides, never use slides for longer than 20 minutes, and never create a slide with a font size smaller than 30. Additional advice from us is to use powerful and compelling images captured with a high-quality camera, and make sure the files are at least 1MB in size. A blurry image is death to a slide presentation.

If you are using videos, work to make them high-quality as well. You have a much better chance of getting great visuals and sound if you use a good camera and microphone. Most smartphones are good enough, though, particularly if you plug in a basic microphone. The golden rule, established by MTV (maybe), is to keep your videos under four minutes.

If your entire team are amateurs at design, it is worth investing the time to find someone who knows what they are doing. At the very least, google "great slide decks" for some inspiration, or reach out to some students for their design eye—they might be better at it than many on your team.

RELAX AND GET CENTERED

Before The Talk with your community, your leadership team needs to take a few minutes to chill out. We know, that's a tall order. This is not just any old public speech you are giving.

To help you relax, get to the venue an hour early to get a feel for the room. Also make sure that all your technology works, by which we mean your slides look great on the screen, any videos you plan to show will actually play (and aren't reliant on a streaming internet connection), and your clicker works. Minimizing the chances of technology trouble is a surprisingly effective reassurance tactic.

Then get centered. You are a powerful leadership team, sharing a vision of where the school is heading with an audience who have trusted you to lead them. You love this school, you love this new direction, and you are the team to make it happen—so own it. Remind yourself that this is a great chance to get a whole group of people on board with what you are doing. Tell yourself those aren't nerves you're feeling; that's excitement. You are a Dream Team.

SLOW DOWN

You probably *will* be excited. And this is all the more reason to make sure that while you are up on that stage, you speak slowly—both to be heard and to achieve the impact you want to achieve.

As an exercise, watch a few minutes of the "I Have a Dream" speech and notice the pace that Martin Luther King Jr. uses. While it feels incredibly slow when you hear him, it has become the most well-known speech in history.

He got his message across. Make sure you do the same.

DON'T DRAG IT OUT

You don't need to give a 90-minute speech to wow an audience. Consider that TED gives its speakers just two rules: *You have 17 minutes. Be profound.*

Our best guidance for your team is that when you get up in front of your community for The Talk, speak with honesty and clarity, and then get off the stage. Be sincere, be brief, and be seated.

If you are still not convinced on this point, think of the last wedding you attended. Maybe a grandmother stood up and said, "I love my granddaughter, and I am so happy that you met the love of your life. May your life together be filled with happiness, just like mine was with my wonderful husband." Now that is an incredible wedding speech. Contrast that with drunk Uncle Robert (we all have a family member like this), who grabbed the microphone and went on for 20 minutes. Grandma was sincere and brief, and then she got off the stage. Be like Grandma.

KEEP YOUR BODY LANGUAGE IN CHECK

We have done presentation training with school leadership teams around the world, and it is incredible what we have seen people do when they are nervous. Earrings, watches, rings, pinky fingers, thighs, and noses all get abused when people are losing their confidence in front of an audience.

The easiest way to stop yourself from fidgeting—and thus, distracting your audience and undermining your credibility—is to hold your hands out in front of you, almost like you are about to catch a basketball. We also call this "T. *rex* arms." It might feel awfully weird at first but it looks fine. In fact, if you watch video of the world's best speakers, it's exactly what they do.

PLAN WHERE YOU'LL STAND

Standing behind a lectern is a great way to disconnect from your audience. Avoid it at all costs.

Lecterns are for academics and for preachers. They're a place for notes or a script. Show your parents and teachers that you respect them enough and understand your ideas so well that you don't need that traditional "authority" marker or a script. If you do need prompts, have some bullet points written in a big font, or have a laptop on stage that you can glance down at. If you can take your speaking to a notes-free level, your message will come across far more powerfully.

This is not permission to run around the stage like Mick Jagger, though. Plan to stay in one spot for about three-quarters of the talk and move around a little bit from there. Another option is to set up a few stools for you and other members of the leadership team. It's a great way to illustrate that your team is united and approachable.

BE CONFIDENT

When your team shares your story and your vision as leaders, the goal is to come across as the most confident people in the room. Stand up with confidence; open with confidence; continue with confidence. If you are someone who sweats when you are nervous, choose your outfit carefully (or invest a few extra dollars in a really good antiperspirant). Own the strategy and own your mandate as leaders.

CLOSE BRILLIANTLY

Make it a goal to leave people on a high, feeling inspired or feeling contemplative. We recommended starting with a story, and we recommend ending with one too. If you are really creative, you can conclude The Talk with the ending of the story that you started at its beginning.

Blow their socks off. Make them cry. Make them all want to join your cause. There is a big difference between a speech that people react to with a "Nice speech!" and one that gets everyone on their feet saying, "Let's march!"

you won't please everyone, but that's ok

Change is hard work, and you need big shoulders to lead it as a team.

You will upset people. Some may hate you. Some teachers may quit. Some parents may withdraw their children. Expect to encounter some gossip, cold e-mails, and even straight-out lies. This is normal. Do not take it to heart.

Dave used to have a rule in his leadership teams that he called "80 percent." It was that if 80 percent of the school community liked the leadership team, they were doing OK, ensuring that the 20 percent who didn't were not always the same people. This approach affords you the emotional license necessary to continue to make big, bold, and important decisions.

We also refer to the likeability credits that we can use as leaders as "clutch credits." Use your clutch credits when you have something really important to get done but will need to upset a few people to achieve it. Essentially, this is when you say, "I have been really great to you for a while, and this request might upset you, but I really need your help here." If some of your team are low on clutch credits after pushing though a whole bunch of tough asks, it's time for other members of the team to step up and cash in some of theirs. On a Dream Team, there's no room for a popularity contest as to who the most-liked leader is. On a Dream Team, it's about everyone pitching in to get the job done.

With all this said, yes, it is important for your team to keep the voices of outliers and objectors in perspective. The leadership team at Bayview had a 95 percent response rate to an important survey that they put out. When they presented the new direction the school was moving in regarding the school's name change, 85 percent of the community voted in favor. Yet there was a small minority of parents who felt more comfortable with the past than with the new direction. There was a feeling among them that the new leadership team was being too ambitious and overestimating what it could achieve in areas where past school leaders had been unsuccessful. In Australia, we call this "tall poppy syndrome." It's when the tall poppies—those with ambition and desire—are cut down by those who are shorter. Members of the Bayview leadership team *were* very optimistic, and this didn't sit well with everyone. But the grumbling quieted when the results started coming through.

To borrow some phrasing from Teddy Roosevelt, it is not the critic who counts—not the person who points out how the strong one stumbles or where the doer of deeds could have done them better; the credit belongs to the leadership teams who are in the arena. And if your team needs additional advice on the matter, we like this, from our good friends at KIPP Infinity in Harlem: "Forgive yourselves every night and recommit every morning." Then there's this, from the famously offensive Scottish comedian Billy Connelly: "F--k the begrudgers."

So now that you have prepared your school community and partners for the change, you need to work to get the culture right in preparation for moving into solution mode.

6
LEADERSHIP EXPANSION

How can we enlist more leaders throughout the school to support this change?

A decade ago, Perth was a boomtown.

A thousand kilometers north of the city, in the Pilbara region of Western Australia, massive yellow machines had been tearing iron ore out of the red dust and packing boats to the brim with the stuff to send to a Chinese economy hungry for more. Unskilled workers willing to live in blisteringly hot mining towns in basic camp accommodations could earn hundreds of thousands of dollars a year doing even the most basic tasks. Working on three-weeks-on/one-week-off turnarounds, the miners would return to Perth with hefty bank balances. Many spent their fortunes on new cars, jet skis, exotic holidays, and sky-high bar tabs.

It felt like a new Gold Rush, but as quickly as it came, it was gone. The Chinese stopped buying the iron ore, the building works slowed to a halt, and the companies stopped hiring. Unskilled jobs were the first to go, but soon after, even qualified engineers found themselves competing with 200 people for a single job opening.

Back in the city, the changes were felt hardest in places like Armadale, 30 kilometers away from the air-conditioned boardrooms of the publicly listed mining companies. Its suburban streets read like an autobiography, with cars bought on credit resting on bricks, unregistered and baking in the hot sun. Front gardens that were once carefully landscaped had become dusty and overgrown. With the unemployment rate as high as 20 percent in recent years, Armadale has more welfare recipients than any community in the state. It also holds the unenviable titles of the city's top location for assault and car theft. The story here may remind some of many others playing out across the Rust Belt of the United States.

Understandably, teaching at Armadale's public, 900-student Challis Community Primary School comes with its challenges.

When Principal Lee Musumeci first arrived, she knew that a traditional model of schooling wasn't working. She also knew that in such a tough learning situation, the familiar leadership structure of principal, deputies, and heads of department wasn't going to work either. Challis needed more leaders, and leaders throughout the school. So Lee assembled Challis's "18 leaders," a group of instruction- and transformation-minded colleagues willing to give their all. It was the only way, she thought, for Challis to have any chance of achieving ambitious goals.

building a team to go the distance

The African proverb says, "If you want to go fast, go alone, but if you want to go far, go together."

In the first five chapters of this book, we have focused on the small "core team" of leaders and the work they must do to lead a change effort in a school. This includes listening to their students, fellow staff members, and community members; focusing on the school's top challenges and opportunities; figuring out a new direction for the school; and boldly articulating that direction for the rest of the school's stakeholders. As you move to Step 6 of the Change Leader Journey, however, it's time to make a cultural shift, and that means expanding your team.

Every school we profile in this book had an exceptional principal whom many credited with leading the school's change effort. Yet when questioned about the key change leaders in their school, all of these principals were quick to point to their deputies and then to the larger distributed leadership teams that were built over the years. All these distributed leadership teams had processes and systems that allowed for highly effective collaboration, better solutions to problems, and a more sustainable organization.

Building up these distributed leadership teams isn't easy, however. All these Dream Team core leaders spent years identifying and fine-tuning the right talent, processes, and structures for their schools. Here is what they did—and what you can do too.

HAVE THE COURAGE TO SHAKE THINGS UP

In the early years of the transformation efforts, none of the Dream Teams hesitated to let school staff know that there would be changes ahead and that these changes would reach even the most senior levels of leadership. As Manurewa Intermediate School's Iain Taylor put it, "We had to clean out the cupboard." In his opinion, change was needed, rapidly, and in his first term as principal, Iain devised a plan for all middle managers to relinquish their positions in advance of an entirely new management structure. These certainly weren't popular moves, but he felt the situation was so dire that an injection of new, higher expectations and a feeling of urgency was crucial. Some may see this kind of leadership as heavy-handed, but several schools, particularly those closest to crisis, found bold, top-down decisions the best choice in those early days. As the deputy principal at Lesher Middle School, a former National Guard captain, told us, "It was a case of bottom-up when possible, but top-down when necessary."

At Bayview Secondary College, the leadership team felt that they had the right individuals on their team but that some of these individuals were in the wrong roles. "It was completely disjointed," Principal Gill Berriman laughed. Luckily, she was in a strong position to shake things up: all of Bayview's leaders, herself included, were performing their roles on an "acting" basis. Gill focused on reshuffling leaders across the school and set to work moving her individuals around, much like a coach on a soccer field.

In your school, how bold do you think you can be, or need to be? Are there some major shifts that you want to make early to demonstrate to your community that you are serious and that the school is open to making big changes?

FIGURE OUT WHETHER EVERYONE IS STAYING ON THE BUS

Some Dream Teams were willing to clean house, and others were eager to keep everyone and make things work with the people they had.

At Challis, the leadership team was quick to encourage staff members not aligned to the vision to move on. Some took early retirement or transferred to different schools; others remained on staff but were shifted to positions that had less influence on the new improvement agenda. Following the district's turnaround policies, Lindsa McIntyre and the team at Jeremiah E. Burke High School had to re-interview all of their staff and let half of them go. At Manurewa, after a formal assessment of all teachers and leaders in the school, Iain determined that many staff were underperforming. He saw several explanations for this—the first being that 22 of the school's 28 teachers were provisional and in either their first few years of teaching or their first few years of teaching in New Zealand. Interestingly, 17 of the 22 provisional teachers were immigrant teachers from India, South Africa, or Fiji. This is usually no problem whatsoever, but by their own admission, these Manurewa teachers were overwhelmed by the unfamiliar cultural challenge of teaching the school's Maori and Pacific Island children. Principal Iain Taylor remembers with sadness a situation where he decided to let one such teacher go early in the transformation of the school. He drove her home that afternoon, and as he pulled up to her home, she thanked him with tears in her eyes, expressing relief that she was out of the school.

While it is certainly not a pleasant situation for anyone, some leadership teams made the tough decision to part ways with underperforming staff members, and this is an option your team may want to consider (one that is not without its challenges). In all the schools that went this route, the parting was done with grace and as the last step in a process of heightened internal accountability and relevant instructional support.

To get a clearer sense of who is eager to be part of the change process ahead, it can be helpful to have in-depth discussions with every member of your staff to see how they are personally reacting. Another activity you may want to try is to ask all staff, "Which member of the staff do you get the most positive energy from, and which do you learn the most from?" This can help you to map the positive energizers and the most effective instructional leaders in the school, which can be a quick way to identify your most valuable players.

GET CREATIVE WITH STRUCTURES

Many of the schools we spent time with dreamed up new organizational structures and made them work through a combination of clever accounting and the habit of asking for forgiveness more often than they asked for permission. Indeed, many of the Dream Team leaders became animated when they shared their staffing strategies, which saw them moving around roles, choosing not to rehire certain positions, and redirecting buckets of money to new leadership portfolios. Luckily for many of them, as their schools started to thrive, enrollment numbers increased, allowing them greater levels of funding and some degree of autonomy around the new staff they were able to bring into the learning environment.

As mentioned earlier, Challis is led by a senior leadership team of a principal and deputies working in collaboration with a larger group of

18 leaders known, conveniently, as "the 18 leaders." The 18 leaders spend 80 percent of their time in the classroom and the other 20 percent on instructional and transformational leadership activities. But there are other creative ways to meet leadership challenges beyond adding more names to the formal list of leaders. At Wooranna Park Primary School, the leadership structure is tiny: one principal and two deputies. There are no lead teachers, no heads of department; instead, every member of the staff is considered a leader and empowered to step up with autonomy in key areas.

To help you shake up the leadership structure in your school, try to innovate some new structures that aren't visually represented by the classic leader at the top, line managers under them, and then people sitting in different departments. Also consider whether you can change around some job titles. Freeing yourself from the traditional titles (e.g., principal, assistant/deputy principal, head teacher, department head) and the familiar expectations and associations that come with them can be liberating and open up innovation.

UNEARTH HIDDEN TALENT

Have you seen the film *Moneyball*? Brad Pitt plays Billy Beane, the real-life general manager of the Oakland Athletics. Unable to compete with the richer clubs in Major League Baseball, Beane worked with a Harvard-educated statistician (played by Jonah Hill) to use sabermetric principles to run his team. The new roster they put together surprised many, including some players who lost their positions, fans who had come to expect a certain type of team, and MLB experts and commentators. In the face of this criticism, the Oakland A's went on to win 20 games in a row the next year and have one of their most successful seasons in recent history.

In many ways, the majority of the leadership teams that we profiled for *Dream Team* took an Oakland A's approach. Without the luxury of paying high salaries to recruit whoever they would like, they needed to uncover passionate and intelligent members of staff who were well aligned with where the school was headed. As they say at Lesher Middle School, they were looking for "character and competence." The Lesher team used these simple criteria as a basis to hire new staff members, encourage others to move on, promote some people internally into leadership positions, and shift leaders who weren't thriving back into purely instructional roles.

We found another great example of a Billy Beane–style leadership selection at Bayview, where the core leadership team tapped for their community education coordinator a physical education teacher who, rather bizarrely, was serving as the head of the math department at the beginning of the transformation effort. In this important leadership role, he was responsible for one of the team's three focus areas. "He's our Ideas Man," Principal Gill Berriman told us, "and he is the visionary who has raised our external profile and innovated many internal approaches that have changed our learning environment." Gill and her leadership team also saw untapped potential in a young teacher in his first year at Bayview, whom they appointed as an advanced skills teacher to work with the school's most challenging kids. He thrived in the role, and the kids thrived as a result.

The leadership team at the Burke made some similar unconventional draft picks. Principal Lindsa McIntyre explained, "We had a plan. We then needed to get the right team." Lindsa looked for doers, "exceptional people with things they wanted to get done." The majority of new team members she found were not established leaders; in fact, some of them were not even established educators. Artis Street, for example, was an electrical engineer with an MBA who had been thriving in the corporate sector. Unable to ignore the passion he had to make a difference for children, he moved into education. Lindsa and the leadership team at the Burke were quick to identify Artis as a key talent and acted immediately to bring him in as an instructional leader in the school. Cheryl Windle was a social worker with only a few years of experience at the Burke who had been overlooked for leadership positions in the past. When the core leadership decided to make a dramatic strategic swing toward educating the whole child and supporting trauma-informed practices, Cheryl's skills were exactly what they needed. They brought her into a senior leadership role, where she has stayed throughout the transformation.

At John Polanyi Collegiate Institute in Toronto, the leadership team conducted a quick overall assessment of the staff and divided their performances into three tiers. Their rough numbers showed that 20 percent of the staff were outstanding—passionate educators who were getting great results and consistently working to better themselves and their students; they would be strong supporters of the change effort. (In fact, the leadership team decided that this top 20 percent—five teachers—were responsible for 80 percent of what was great about the school.) The next tier of performers—60 percent of the staff—were mid-level performers. They were mostly effective educators who had room to improve in some areas but might get on board with and contribute to the new strategic direction, given the right support. (This was the tier that the leadership team decided to focus the majority of their efforts on, hoping to win their commitment and unleash their creativity and effort.) The final 20 percent were seen as the least effective, the neediest, and often the loudest. Knowing the minimal returns on getting blood from a stone, the team devoted little time and effort to recruiting staff members in this tier for the leadership effort.

At Challis, on the other side of the world, the core leadership team took two years to build out the foundation of their 18 leaders concept. Their major focus was bringing in instructional leaders who were positively disposed to the research-grounded, best-practice approaches they were pushing. And they started looking in unconventional places. For example, Kristy Tomlinson joined the school as a speech pathologist; after showing excellence, winning several awards, and demonstrating her commitment to the Challis way, she was promoted to coordinator of student services. She has remained in this role for years, leading the extended service programs that have put Challis on the global map for taking innovative approaches to early childhood learning.

At your school, another approach you could take is to draw some inspiration from the idea of a sports-style draft. If you asked each member of your leadership team to pick out some "prospects" who are impressive but inexperienced in the top leagues of leadership, you might get a quick sense of whom people have had their eye on. It is also worth considering running a "pathway to leadership" fast-track program, where up-and-coming leaders can apply to be part of a structured learning experience within the school.

AIM FOR A MIX OF FRIENDS AND STRANGERS

This is a simple point, but it is often overlooked by leadership teams in the interest of fostering coherence and unity. Recruiting your friends—people you have worked with in the past—definitely has its upsides. Iain Taylor drew on this tactic at Manurewa when he needed to quickly populate his leadership team with people he could expect to be both professional and pragmatic. He knew everyone would get along and work together harmoniously.

But sometimes, too much peace can have a soporific effect. You need a clash of minds to review new angles and new solutions. The fact is, devil's advocates, as frustrating as they can be to leaders who want to get things done, can offer opinions that simply aren't heard in a culture of yes.

At John A. Leslie, the core leadership team made it standard practice to bring in colleagues who would challenge them. As Principal Greg McLeod shared with us, "You find your allies for sure, but then you have to seek out the people who are almost always a counter to us and bring them inside as new allies. We need their insights, and we love it when our ideas clash. That discourse, the challenging, the fighting—it is all vital to our success."

We ourselves believe that if everyone on a team agrees all the time, then half of them might as well go home. When we cofounded Education Changemakers, we came from very different backgrounds, and our new staff members would laugh about how much we argued. But we encouraged them to watch strategy meetings closely and notice that yes, we argued, sometimes fiercely, but by the end of the meeting, we had always come to an agreement. And we were always as solid as oak behind that agreement, knowing that we had made it together. One of the mantras we have at EC we learned from our friends at KIPP Infinity: "We are frank, and then we rally."

With this in mind, as a leadership team, ask yourselves whether you need to expand beyond a small circle of friends and introduce greater diversity of voices and insights to your distributed leadership setup. Where will you find these voices? How will you handle challenges to the decisions and directions you've set? How will you come to agreement?

PROMOTE PASSION

Many of the more interesting hires that the Dream Teams made to create their wider distributed leadership teams were individuals who displayed high levels of passion for the work. The team at John A. Leslie started every interview, for both internal and external hires, with a simple question: "Why did you get into education?" Greg McLeod and his vice principal searched for passionate educators and quickly identified two new key lieutenants in their change effort. The first was in her first year of teaching and had studied at the university where Greg had been a lecturer. The other was a teacher who had been at the school for years but had been overlooked for leadership roles. An exceptional educator, and with the skills to share this experience as an instructional leader, she became a powerful force in the John A. Leslie transformation effort.

It was interesting for to us to see how many leadership teams were able to identify very early-stage teachers and fast-track them into positions of influence. To continue with the Oakland A's/Billy Beane analogy, these schools were making good first-round draft picks. At the Burke, the team brought in a number of Teach for America associates, many of whom performed with excellence and remain in the school as leaders today. Of all the 18 leaders that we interviewed at Challis, 17 of them were in their first formal educational leadership role.

Here are some more key questions for your core leadership team to be asking as you build out your distributed network of leaders. Are you effectively tapping into the passion of your teachers? Are you attracting educators who are inspired to make a difference in line with your strategic direction? Are you making time to check in with your staff on how passionate they are about the work?

FIND THE DOERS

Schools run best when they're a mix of *visionaries* (just a few of them are needed, often in the core leadership team), *analysts* (the devil's advocates who can challenge the visionaries), and *doers* (the implementors who are capable of executing the initiatives and making things happen).

For your distributed leadership team, seek out and bring on board as many doers as you can. As John Polanyi's Aiman Flahat says, "When you build that entrepreneurial spirit in people, they mobilize themselves, and it is amazing what can be achieved." Jennie Vine had been a secondary school teacher before she arrived at Wooranna Park Primary School, but the leadership team saw her ability to get things done in a junior school setting and offered her a permanent position. Sixteen years later, Jennie is still there and still making a difference for the students—now as their assistant principal.

In your school, as often as you can, give staff the opportunity to take initiative and make things happen. When Aaron was in the military, he was trained to ensure that whenever he raised an issue with his superiors, he had two solutions already prepared and a clear idea of which one he thought was best. You could also consider providing small grants or periods of time that staff can use to pitch or work on projects they care about.

MAKE SURE THERE'S A DECISIVE LEADER AT THE TOP

With all this talk of distributing leadership throughout the school, it's important to point out that everyone needs to know that the buck still stops with the core leadership team.

While we saw great examples of distributed leadership at all of the schools we spent time with for *Dream Team*, the core leaders—and the principals, in particular—still had the final say. The USA's National Association of Secondary School Principals (NASSP) named Lesher's principal, Tom Dodd, 2017 National Principal of the Year. Yes, he was known for his supportive leadership style, but we heard several members of the team comment that "the final decision rests with Tom." A senior leader at Challis spoke of Lee Musumeci, the 2011 Australian Primary Principal of the Year, as the team's inspiration. "We have our 18 leaders, and that is key for us, but Lee picks out the areas that we need to develop, and we go and make that happen."

So even as you work to distribute democratic leadership throughout the school, make sure that everyone understands that your core leadership team—and your principal, at the pointy end—has the final say and will be accountable for the team's collective decisions. And if you're that principal, you have to be willing to take in the information, evaluate the options, make that "captain's call" when you have to, and of course, deal with the consequences.

MAKE LEADERSHIP DEVELOPMENT A CONSTANT

None of the Dream Teams we spent time with saw their efforts to build out distributed leadership capacity as complete. To them, this was ongoing cultural work, something that the principal and deputies would always need to devote a percentage of their time to, and something that would always be difficult to get right.

Challis is, by all accounts, a challenging place to work. Each year a number of staff do leave—with approximately half not having their contracts renewed, and the other half moving on for personal reasons. Yet with each new hire, the members of Challis's leadership team feel themselves to be closer to achieving the distributed leadership necessary to fully achieve their vision of the school. As we heard many times, when people are hired into "the Challis way" (or "the ChiTech way" or the "ways" of the other

Dream Team schools), the change in progress gets stickier and more sustainable. Initiatives become approaches—no longer notable, just "how things are done here."

It's the same at the Burke, where leadership continues to evolve—particularly as some of the strongest core team leaders depart to take over principalships elsewhere in the Cambridge Public School system. It's a bittersweet pattern. Principal Lindsa McIntyre consistently taps new talent on the shoulder, believing that everyone can be a leader and that it is usually only fear that holds people back from stepping up as educators. She works to remove that fear in Burke's safe and supportive environment.

She also invests heavily in her team.

A PhD-degreed educator in her own right, Lindsa encourages the core members of her team to complete master's and doctoral programs, and she works to provide them with high-quality professional development opportunities and rapid promotion. She pointed out that when staff members feel like they are still growing and learning, they stay . . . at least until they are poached to lead their own schools!

As a leadership team, take a moment to audit what leadership development is happening, both for you and for other members of the staff. Also work to ensure that while instructional leadership is being prioritized, transformational leadership aimed at improving learning and whole-school performance receives a powerful investment of time and resources.

the power and agency of human beings

Before we move on from distributed leadership, please excuse a brief foray into philosophy.

At the end of the days we spent with these Dream Teams, we always walked away buoyed by an immense feeling of optimism and hope. At the airport, exhausted from another day of travel, we would recall things we'd heard—statements from team members about their school, their students, and one another. Almost always we found ourselves thinking, *These people are great humans.*

We started asking the leaders if they would agree that there was a touch of humanism about them. Almost always, they would nod and smile. For those who might not know, *humanism* is defined as a life approach that emphasizes the value and agency of human beings, both individually and collectively. Essentially, humanists see great potential in people and do their part to bring out that potential. We see this humanism as an approach that integrates naturally with all kinds of more traditional spiritualities and religious principles.

Humanism veritably shone out of Aiman Flahat, the recently retired principal of John Polanyi. "Some of my teachers were angels," he told us. "They would spend their weekends with kids—tutoring, at games, and supporting parents." Aiman would walk the halls every day, making sure that his teachers knew he was there and that he appreciated them. He knew that if there was trust, credibility, and relationship among the team at John Polanyi, that they could achieve great things. And that's what they did.

So to recap as we come to the end of Chapter 6, as a leadership team you have now

1. Honestly and powerfully aligned your passions for change.
2. Spent important time listening to key members of your school community to help you understand the problems worth solving.
3. Distilled these insights to no more than three key areas that you are going to focus on.
4. Worked to achieve the autonomy you need from system leaders, and provided them with the alignment they need to be comfortable.
5. Engaged and inspired your school community around the directions that have been decided upon.

6. Discovered more leaders across the school to more powerfully drive this change.

Now we get to one of the most important steps in the Change Leader Journey: fostering the innovative culture that will actually create the solutions to the problems you have decided to solve.

7
CULTURE

How can we foster an innovative culture and generate new ideas for solving identified problems?

Principal Greg McLeod entered his office at John A. Leslie Public School, coffee cup in hand. He had just completed a walk of the building, a daily practice devoted to chatting with children and staff and looking and listening for anything left unsaid.

Greg sat down heavily in his chair, placed his cup next to his computer mouse, and got ready to read through some of the e-mails he had saved from his early morning admin blast. There was an iPad resting on top of his keyboard with a sticky note attached to its screen. *Play Me!* the note commanded.

With a grin, Greg peeled off the sticker, powered up the device, and then pressed play on the video he found waiting for him. It was a three-minute idea pitch from the school's grade 1 class. They had been working with the grade 4s across the hall and were envious of the innovative learning space that the older students had managed to set up (building much of the furniture themselves, in a nod to the tight budget).

In the video, the grade 1s made a strong argument: a new learning environment would allow them to self-regulate more effectively, give them more innovation spaces when they needed to work together, and provide quieter areas for personal work. They listed the furniture they would like, how much it would all cost, and the time lines they were willing to follow to make it happen.

Over the past few years, the leadership team at John A. Leslie had been working very hard to instill a culture of learning, problem solving, and innovation in the school. Seeing it so well represented by 6-year-olds was a breakthrough. *We are good,* thought Greg, nodding and smiling. *We are solid.* Within a month, the grade 1s had their new class design.

Yet only a few years earlier, John A. Leslie School was not a place anyone would have described as innovative. When Greg took over as principal, "the school was stuck in a certain point in time, and we needed to adapt." It had taken years to change, but the signs of transformation were impossible to ignore. When a retired superintendent paid a visit to the school, she wondered with a smile, "Where do you keep all the *disengaged* kids?" A week after a visit to John A. Leslie, an Ontario deputy assistant minister for education was still buzzing about the school, remarking, "The kids kept grabbing me, wanting to make sure that I saw what they had been working on, and asking for my feedback constantly."

The students that John A. Leslie served when we paid our visit were very different from the students who had attended a few years earlier. For Greg's leadership team, recognition of that demographic shift was an impetus for change. As we mentioned earlier in the book, Greg tried to lead the change himself for the first year. Fresh from his position as a university lecturer, he took a traditional instructional leadership approach, and it fell short. The changes simply weren't coming fast enough. After a brief summer break, Greg kicked off his second year by bringing a core leadership team together. Together, they created strategies to distribute leadership throughout the school and build a community where all staff were confident and capable of solving problems. The goal was to get more done, more effectively.

Over time, John A. Leslie's school theme became "Agents of Change." Every member of the learning community was encouraged to solve problems, and they were given the support, time, and resources to do so. As an example, a teacher once came to Greg with a complaint that a faucet in the grades 2 and 3 combined classroom was leaking. Knowing that a maintenance request to the head office would sit for a year before the issue was rectified, Greg and the teacher decided to throw the challenge to the class. No, the children didn't have the plumbing skills or resources to fix the issue directly, but they did have the ability to recast the problem as an opportunity. They started collecting the excess water and launched a plant watering business in the school. A young group of creatives also launched an artists' network, supplying water to the school's portable classes so the grades 7 and 8 students there could create watercolor paintings for sale and exhibition.

To foster innovation, John A. Leslie's leadership team also launched a new expenses strategy in which any request for spending had to answer three key questions: (1) What do you want? (2) How much will it cost? and (3) How will it improve learning for kids? If the requestor could answer these questions well, leadership would hustle to find the funding. We should note that in all the years this process was used, leadership said yes to every application it received—and the school's overall expenses still went down.

The cultural development experienced at John A. Leslie illustrates both instructional and transformational leadership in action. From an instructional lens, the leadership team worked to bring students to the center of the improvement discussion. They supported the formation of the Student School Improvement Group, which toured classrooms and provided recommendations to teachers and leaders in line with learning goals and success criteria.

When leadership removed the rows of desks from classrooms, replacing them with group tables, the students were quick to say that this measure wasn't enough. One of the student representatives pointed out, "We are so past group work. We innovate and collaborate in different teams, so we just need a bunch of spaces around the school that we can use for a time and move around in." It was the grade 4s who led this shift in classroom environment, which had major ramifications for learning and pedagogy. After the audacious grade 1s demanded this kind of flexible setup for themselves, it became a whole-school approach.

All this innovation, transparency, and collective problem solving and learning was not the way things used to be. Greg told us that during his first month at the school, he was pulled aside by a well-meaning member of the school board. "The other day, you came into the staff room and started talking about school stuff," the board member said. "Well, we have a little rule that we don't talk about education in the staff room." Greg's response was immediate, and it was friendly but firm: "Well, we have a problem then, because education is all I am going to talk about in here."

Greg was as good as his word. He and the leadership team went on to launch the "Doors Open" initiative, in which teachers and leaders could share what they were struggling with in their classrooms—an instructional strategy, classroom management, and so on—and request input and class visits from others. Similarly, staff who felt they were doing something well would share this success and encourage visitors to come see these approaches modeled. Early in the life of this initiative, the school was informed that due to disagreements between the Ontario government and the teachers union, teachers were not allowed to formally meet as a staff at the school. Rather than letting this edict hinder their learning, the teachers created their own workaround that nevertheless adhered to union guidelines: an online sharing platform and class visits scheduled during personal time. As Greg noted, "Teaching can be such an isolating experience, so we needed to open the doors to practice, and all become better instructional leaders together." It worked.

Twitter emerged as a powerful platform for the John A. Leslie teachers, and the core leadership team led the charge by setting up their own personal accounts and taking photos of great learning in action whenever they observed it. What this public outreach did was signal to the teachers and parents and wider community following online the kinds of learning that were valued at the school. As this strategy increased in popularity, teachers began to experience leaders calling after them in the hallway and asking them to come into their class to tweet out an insight into what they were up to—a powerful example of a strong learning community.

This spirit of group problem solving caught on with students as well. They asked for whiteboards to be installed in the hallways and markers to always be available. Members of the learning community used these boards to describe challenges or questions they had; the student body enthusiastically provided responses and solutions. When a parent asked the deputy principal why there was no graffiti in the hallways, even with all the markers around, the deputy replied, "The kids are too busy engaging with the questions to think about graffitiing!"

Most important, the leadership team at John A. Leslie encouraged a schoolwide acceptance of risk taking and experimentation. As principal, Greg led from the front here, stating that as the most senior instructional leader in the school, he was going to try new things, take risks and occasionally fail. His weekly public musings on these efforts gave others a license to try new things too.

The result of all of this cultural change? We will share the actual numbers later in the book, but suffice it to say, if John A. Leslie's problem was that it hadn't changed in decades, by the time the new innovation culture was fully embedded, that particular problem had been well and truly solved.

preparing for the innovating

About now, you may be thinking, *Hey! This was supposed to be an* innovation *book. Why haven't we gotten to the innovating part yet?*

We've very deliberately made you wait for it, and there are two reasons why.

First, it is vitally important that innovators spend sufficient time finding out what the problems they need to address are and digging down to understand these problems. The innovators and entrepreneurs in the world who succeed are those who start with a problem and work toward a solution, rather than those who come up with ideas randomly and try to force them down people's throats. Einstein once said, "Give me an hour to solve a problem, and I will spend 55 minutes trying to understand the problem, and 5 minutes coming up with my solution."

Second, you can't simply ask your staff to "think outside the box" and then sit back and watch the innovations flow. Without the right environment, staff will struggle to be vulnerable with each other, to come up with new ideas, to try things, to work on their weaknesses, and to become powerful transformational and instructional leaders. Instead, you need to ensure that your culture is defined by innovation and learning. And that takes time and some great leadership, and we are looking at you to make this happen.

So here at Step 7—one of the most significant steps in the Change Leader Journey—we will share some tools you can use to do just that. We'll draw on our own experiences, pass on ideas that we have picked up around the world, and take a peek at how the Dream Teams that we spent time with got things done.

And just to up the stakes, we want you to read the rest of the chapter with this caution in mind: *If you want your school's culture to be an innovative one and it's not, this is probably your team's fault, because you are the culture makers.* Yes, the stakes are high, so you need to do this right. But with the tools in the next few chapters, plus a few tools that you come up with yourself, the challenges will be much easier to meet.

creating an environment for innovation

Before we go deeper into the tools, let's look at what it takes to get into the right mindset and lay the foundation for fruitful school-focused innovation.

KEEP KIDS AS THE FOCUS

Never forget that the kids are what it is all about.

All of the Dream Teams we spent time with had this as the foundation of their innovation culture. They all had different ways of coming up with ideas and solving problems, but the question they always returned to was "What will this do for kids?" Try to do the same!

MAKE SURE EVERYONE IS WILLING TO TAKE RISKS

The word *everyone* is vital here.

A trap that many schools fall into is building small innovation teams who are tasked with coming up with new ideas. Remember, as a leadership team, it's your responsibility to foster innovation, learning, and risk taking across the entire organization—from the librarian to the maintenance team, from the financial controllers to the art teachers, and from the students to the chairperson of your parent-teacher association. While some Dream Teams we met did appoint an individual to lead on innovation or organizational learning, this person's role was always to act as a facilitator of ideas, not the sole creator. At Manurewa Intermediate School, the mantra "All the time, every time, all of us, everywhere" is a powerful example of this. At the Burke, they espouse the same idea repeatedly: building a better school is a case of "All hands on deck."

As we talked about earlier, Greg at John A. Lesle started a blog where he documented the things that he was working on and gave updates on what worked, what didn't, and the lessons learned. This is public, accountable risk taking. Want some nonschool examples? We heard of a company that had a large glass container in its lobby. When staff members initiated a new innovation, they put a clear marble in the container. If the idea worked, they returned to the lobby container and dropped a colored marble inside. There were far more clear marbles than colored ones in that container. In the tech industry, there is a culture of "F--k Up Nights," where entrepreneurs share their biggest failures and what they learned from them. An important message here, though, is that ultimate failure is not great. No educator wants to tell a school community that their school has failed and is being shut down, just as no business entrepreneur wants to tell their staff and investors that they are bankrupt and it is all over. Ultimately, success is the goal, even though a few trip-ups and an occasional face-plant are expected parts of the journey.

Building a schoolwide culture of risk taking is much easier said than done, and for every leadership team we meet that has achieved this, we see 10 who are merely paying lip service to the idea. Because risk taking is scary. The chances of failure are high. But doing nothing is a sure fail.

At Jeremiah E. Burke High School, the team knows that the work they do is difficult. They encourage new ideas via the mantra "Failure is feedback for success," which we heard across the school, from leaders at all levels. At Chicago Tech Academy High School—which, like the Burke, educates kids who are growing up in a tough urban setting—Assistant Principal Tiara Wheatley works to ensure that all staff know that they can "explore things and make mistakes. They just have to learn from them and tell the team about the lessons they gathered." When everyone has an understanding that "if we succeed or fail, we do it together," the sense of loyalty and unity is palpable.

BE HONEST ABOUT YOUR WEAKNESSES

Another thing we noticed in our travels to schools around the world for *Dream Team* was the strong trends associated with instructional leadership. There was a prevalent narrative that the principal and the layer of leaders immediately under the principal needed to be the most accomplished instructional coaches in the building. The meta-analyses of John Hattie (2009) tell us there is academic and theoretical merit to this approach. However, we saw the risk of decreased transparency and vulnerability across a leadership team when leaders were afraid to admit they were not totally expert across all of the school's instructional areas.

The most successful instructional leaders we met were not afraid to acknowledge this publicly. John A. Leslie's Greg McLeod said, for example, "As the most senior instructional leader in the building, I am OK to admit that I am not good at these things and would like support to get better at them." At John Polanyi Collegiate Institute, Aiman Flahat got excited when he talked about increasing the leadership team's willingness to be open to vulnerability. During our conversation with him late into the evening, he put down his wine glass and leaned forward as he told us, "I said to the team, please tell me what you are struggling with, what you want to learn. Maybe education is the only profession where you can do that; it is amazing." Aiman said that when he was honest about being the top instructional leader who was still trying to get better, he saw positive changes in the school's learning culture. At the Burke, the team had to work hard to shift the perception that a classroom visit from another teacher or leader was a sign of weakness. Lindsa McIntyre explained that she is careful to make sure her team understands that anyone can be observed at any time. "Don't stress if we walk into your room," she tells them.

HAVE A BIAS FOR YES

Many of the Dream Teams we spent time with had a bias for yes.

At Lesher Middle school in Colorado, Principal Tom Dodd said his team's approach to decision making was "unless there is a policy violation or an equity issue, the answer will be a yes." Cheryl Windle, a team leader at the Burke, was equally clear on this: "We believe in the team, and as leaders, we never say no to an idea. If a teacher says, 'I think we should do boxing and I am going to lead the boxing program,' then I guess we are having boxing at the Burke." At Challis Community Primary School in Perth, a math leader told us, in a very Australian manner, "If you want to have a crack at something, we will find the resources." Jennie Vine, at Wooranna Park Primary School in Melbourne, summed up their decision-making process very quickly: "It is a yes if you can tell us what you want to do, show us your plan to test it out, back it up with a bit of research showing it might work, and make sure it doesn't cost too much or won't get us in too much trouble." The team at Bayview Secondary College actively invited their community to innovate by repeating a very simple line at planning meetings: "What could we be if there was nothing to stop us?"

Is your team's bias for yes as clear and as strong as it is at these schools? Do all members of your school community know what elements they must address or cover to get a yes to the ideas they bring?

BUILD PROCESSES TO SUPPORT INNOVATION AND LEARNING

Across the Dream Teams, we saw a universal dislike for bureaucracy but a common love for systems. At Manurewa in Auckland, Sam Holt talked through the systems and structures they built to foster innovation and learning. He noted in particular the advisory teams constructed to help people get through administrative tasks. For example, if a learning approach a teacher wanted to try had elements of outdoor risk attached, an efficiency team would support them to move through the relevant process. "If you don't make people jump through hoops to get things done, they will achieve more," Sam said. In their book *Coherence* (2015), Michael Fullan and Joanne Quinn share an example of the Hawaii Department of Education, which created a task team instructed to reduce bureaucracy by 25 percent. Within a year, the department had reduced it by double that amount.

Similarly, at Lesher, Tom Dodd stated repeatedly that "high expectations need to be matched with high support." And here's how a leader at Challis described the process that their 18 leaders use to work together:

> *If things are not working, amongst the leaders we will talk through the challenges. People are in tune with each other, and there isn't a culture of blame or finger pointing. There is an acknowledgment that every strategy you try is probably not going to be right the first time. There is a lot of passion and love here, a great community aspect to it all.*

In a similar vein, many of the Dream Teams attempted to shield their staff from complex bureaucracy or other system directions that would undermine the change effort. At Lesher, Tom would tell his staff, "There are things that I am not going to bother you with. We need you focused on the kids." Aiman Flahat said his approach at John Polanyi was to own the complications coming down from the system. When he needed to share certain system directives with staff, he was careful not to create a sense of "us and them"; his approach was simply to state what the directive was and how the school would be aligning itself with it. At Challis, Lee Musumeci constantly found herself shielding the team from commands that came from higher up. She reframed them in "Challis language," and when the system asked for outcomes that were misaligned with her school's priorities, she pushed back with gusto. Greg McLeod fought to keep his team at John A. Leslie on target, and that meant saying no to the district all the time. He said it was part of his job to ensure the leadership team members were not like squirrels—constantly chasing new nuts rather than focusing on the core strategy that they had decided upon.

At your school, could you do a systems audit with the goal of identifying the most and least efficient processes you have in the school and generating ideas for new approaches? You might also consider simply asking staff, "What holds you back from innovating more?" Their answers could highlight some quick wins you can implement immediately or direct you to deeper cultural shifts that you need to support.

MAKE TIME TO GET BETTER AND TRY THINGS

Ask a teacher what they really need, and you'll usually get variations on the same answer. It is rarely "money," or "respect," or "a renovated office." What almost every educator wants most is more time.

If you're in the classroom now, you know how easy it is to get overwhelmed by the constant demands of planning, instructing, reporting, and the myriad other tasks you are expected to complete every day. If you are no longer in the classroom, take a moment to remember what that was like. So when leadership teams announce to school staff that it's time to come up with innovative ideas, heaping yet more work on them, it's understandable that staff members' fingers—often the middle one particularly—tend to get itchy.

To foster innovation, risk taking, and learning throughout your school, you need to set aside time for everyone to truly engage with it.

ChiTech provided a powerful example of building in devoted time for innovation and learning. The entire instructional team meets for almost an hour every morning before students arrive. The Monday meeting kicks off with quick reminders on what the current strategic focuses are and an opportunity for staff to share any new approaches to learning they are experimenting with. On Tuesday, Wednesday, and Thursday, the teachers collaborate on project planning, lesson planning, looking at student work, and brainstorming new ideas. Fridays are focused on reflections and planning as a group. When we asked multiple leaders and staff members at ChiTech whether having all these meetings wasn't overkill, the response was unanimous and united: they loved having the time to connect, share, and enjoy one another's company. Some told us directly that in such a challenging context, and in what can be a very lonely profession, the meetings kept them going.

At Manurewa, the core leaders meet every Monday for five hours, deliberately focusing on mentoring, problem solving, transparent data tracking, and honest communication about who needs help and what help is needed. There is an open-door policy, and other leaders in the wider leadership team are often invited in to present and take part in decisions.

It's notable to us that none of the Dream Team schools making time for innovation and learning are particularly well-resourced. Rather than relying on hiring in more capacity, they get creative with their scheduling and staffing, and they just get on with the job of making things work to support their goals. The Burke's Lindsa McIntyre describes it like this:

"To generate will, I need everyone passionate, engaged, and focused. The fastest way to get this culture is by building capacity and by creating the teams and schedules that allow people to work together."

Making time for innovation is invariably complicated, so here's something to try that's fairly simple and very practical: *Frideation*. This portmanteau of "Friday" and "ideation" involves setting aside a block of time—just 20 minutes—each Friday for staff to gather, bring a problem to the group, and ask for solutions and advice.

Something to be clear about here, though, is that we are not suggesting adding more meetings and taking up more of your teachers' time! We are suggesting you make time for innovation with your team—time that may have to be created by canceling a bunch of other meetings that are no longer as important for the change journey ahead.

KEEP THE INSPIRATION UP

Culture should be a constant concern for you as a leadership team, and to quote Ray Kroc, the American entrepreneur who brought McDonald's to scale, you should always be "green and growing, rather than ripe and rotting." Maintaining a sense of urgency and a commitment to continuous improvement is vital.

Lee Musumeci does this at Challis by appealing to the highest ideals of her staff with the line "There are no excuses. If kids are failing, we are responsible for that failure." At the Burke, Lindsa McIntyre brings a clear sense of love to her learning community. You can see it in her words here:

> *This work is difficult, and we need to keep generating will. So I bring my whole heart to the work every day. Sure, I can give nice speeches and tell people that I love them, but it's more important that I can create [a center of] psychological safety, where we all know that we have each other's backs . . . where we have this opportunity to inquire, to ask, to research, and ultimately, to get better—together.*

In your school, your leadership team should be creative in coming up with ways that you can keep inspiration high across your school, and ensure that this is done frequently, powerfully, and in a way that the staff responds to best.

the innovating part

So now that we have talked through how we create the environment for innovation and learning, we will share a process for actually innovating all of the solutions that you need to the strategic problems that you have identified. Here's a list of what you need to get started.

- *The ideation rules in the next few pages.* These are tools, really—simple to learn, easy to teach to others, and (we think) massively effective.
- *A team.* Around five people to start is perfect. You can innovate as a core leadership team or bring together different teams to innovate. The more diverse your teams, the better, so consider creating teams with a mix of students, parents, staff, leaders, and volunteers.
- *Paper.* Sticky notes work great, but the budget-minded could just cut regular paper into smaller squares, about three inches by three inches.
- *Pens or pencils.* One for each person.
- *Feet.* People think better (and have better energy) if they ideate while they are standing up.
- *Music.* Play some music! Music is scientifically proven to boost creativity.

IDENTIFY YOUR "HOW CAN WE . . . ?" QUESTIONS

As you shift now into a solutions mindset, you need to decide on a few "how can we" questions based on the strategic priorities that you established early in the Change Leader Journey. These are based on the root causes that you circled on your root cause trees (Step 4) and then shared with your community (Step 5).

So let's say that one of the big problems that you identified through listening to your community (Step 2) is that "the community didn't think that the school was very good." (Yes, we recommend you keep things that simple.) Perhaps you came up with many reasons this problem exists, including bad press, an outdated building, an ugly school uniform, and a recent increase in violence in the school. But let's say the root cause that you circled was "The school doesn't prepare kids for a positive future."

Flipping this into a "how can we" question is as simple as saying, "How can we better prepare our students for a positive future?"

Remember that you have up to three strategic priorities that you are working on here, so pause right now to identify your three "how can we" questions. Once you have these clear, write them down on paper or a whiteboard, because these three questions are going to be asked a lot in the school.

LEARN AND FOLLOW THE IDEATION RULES

Our rules for ideation may be familiar to you if you've read our book *Edupreneur*. If your leadership teams (core and distributed) can get comfortable working by these rules, you will be able to come up with loads of great solutions. Note that for the process to work, you do need to follow *all* the rules, so take some time to prepare in advance, and when you bring others into your innovation teams, explain everything clearly. When we use these five rules in schools, first we teach them; then we present a problem to be solved; then we very clearly state, "Ideation rules are now in force"; and only *then* do we start generating ideas.

Rule I: Lots of ideas, please.

Rule 1 is to not stop innovating until you have come up with lots of ideas to solve your "how can we" question. In fact, we don't think you should stop until you have come up with 100 ideas. And before you say, "That will take months to do!" know that the fastest-innovating teams can usually get to 100 ideas in about 20 minutes.

If you want practical tips on how your team can rapidly generate 100 ideas to a specific "how can we" question, we can help:

- Get everyone standing up with a handful of sticky notes each and some pens.
- Play some music. Anything jazzy and fun will work fine. Music without vocals is best, as it doesn't distract.
- Have someone clearly state the "how can we" question.
- Start innovating! Every time someone has an idea, they should write it on a sticky note or a piece of paper, and then say it out loud as they put it down in the middle of the table.

The team at design and consulting firm IDEO are the most vocal and well-known advocates for coming up with a quantity of ideas. When they took a moment to review a few decades of innovation rounds, each with at least 100 solutions, they found that ideas 1 to 60 sometimes gave them some interesting results. Ideas 61 to 80 often got pretty crazy, as the team was pushing their creativity. But between ideas 81 and 100, there were often around 6 brilliant ideas that they wanted to move forward with.

A motto of ours is "First idea, worst idea," so with this in mind, commit in your ideation session to coming up with at least 100 solutions to your root cause.

So let's say we are all ideating together, trying to come up with solutions to the "how do we" question posed earlier: "How can we better prepare our students for a positive future?" Let's riff on this one for a moment.

1. Let's see what the best schools in the world are doing.
2. Let's ask the kids what they want to do in the future.
3. Let's look at the jobs that won't exist in the future and discourage the kids from thinking about these.

Three ideas down, 97 ideas to go. This is easy, right?

Rule 2: Crazy ideas, please.

Our second tool of ideating is that we encourage crazy ideas. Nothing is sacred in the ideation phase, and crazy ideas are welcome.

Without further ado, we present some ridiculous solutions to the question, "How can we better prepare our students for a positive future?"

4. Let's encourage the kids to not prepare for a mythical future and instead help them start their own companies now.

5. Let's get in touch with Doc Brown from *Back to the Future*, borrow the DeLorean, and take the kids into the future to see what it is like.

6. Let's redesign our school uniforms to be really futuristic so that we will always feel like we are getting ready for the future.

7. Let's fire any teachers who aren't future focused.

Well! All of these are very decent crazy ideas. And even better, they bring the idea tally to seven. Only 93 to go! Seriously, though: why do we encourage ridiculous ideas? Because sometimes we stumble upon something pretty great.

For example, back in 1943, naval engineer Richard James knocked a spring off his desk and then chuckled to see it "walk" across the floor. Wondering whether kids would chuckle like he did if they saw a spring "walk" like this, he took the plunge and turned it into a toy. He was able to sell more than 300 million "Slinkys" (Fabry, 2015). But Gary Dahl takes the cake (and millions of dollars) for coming up with the Pet Rock. Over drinks at the bar with friends who were complaining about how obligations to care for their pets meant they couldn't go on vacation, Dahl quipped that his pet rock was no hassle at all. He sold more than a million Pet Rocks in the first six months of his company being opened (Woo, 2015).

Once, when we were working with a group of 14-year-olds from a school in a suburb with the highest obesity levels in the state, we asked them, "How could we make sure every kid at your school ate healthy food every day?" After hearing about air-dropped smoothies and swimming pools full of salad, we heard one kid yell, "Let's rip out all of the non-native trees we have now and plant fruit trees instead!" Today, if you walk around this school, you can grab a piece of fruit from the many fruit trees that line the school's grounds. They even produce enough to sell them at the local markets.

So any idea offered during the ideation phase is great. Just get them all written down quickly and keep moving toward 100 solutions.

Rule 3: Say "Yes, and . . ."

Another reason we encourage lots of crazy ideas is that you never know what they might spark in the group. To further encourage your colleagues to pick up those ideas and take them someplace new, Rule 3 is to greet an idea by first saying "Yes," and then building on it by adding an "and": a new idea or a new direction. It's a technique made famous by the comic improvisational geniuses from Second City in Chicago. No one's ideas get shut down, and every idea leads to another one.

So using the "yes, and" approach, we might greet crazy Idea #5 on our list (the *Back to the Future* one) like this: "Yes, and let's do a movie night, show the movie, and then move into future-focused professional development for the staff." That's Idea #8 to add to the list. Or in response to Idea #2 ("Let's ask the kids what they want to do in the future"), we could say, "Yes, and let's get them to create business cards with their names and future job titles. They can put these on their desk during every class." Boom: Idea #9.

With these little "yes, and" adds, our ideas are getting more complex, things are becoming interesting, and we are getting closer to 100.

Rule 4: Use *we*.

Most of you are with us, but we know there might still be a few reading this who are still spinning from (crazy) Idea #7: "Let's fire any teachers who aren't future focused."

If that got you hot under the collar, fair enough. It's people's livelihoods we are talking about with a statement like that, and it would be callous to just throw it out there and not acknowledge that point. However, leaders who are worried about or uncomfortable with an idea someone has put forward shouldn't just shoot it down, because this risks hampering creativity and can discourage contribution.

A good way to navigate this difficulty is to refocus the idea by using the word *we*.

In this example, it might look like, "Let's think about how we could encourage those who aren't future focused in their lessons to explore these ideas more." Or perhaps, "Let's think about what we could we do to share knowledge between our more forward-thinking staff and those who are more traditional."

Using the word *we* like this does a few things for us. It keeps us moving forward and maybe opens up a whole new area of solutions for the team to think up. And it also takes ego out of the innovation team and helps to short-circuit personality-related conflicts that can sometimes be a problem. You don't want people thinking, *I hate that the idea came from Tony, so I don't want it moving forward* or *Margaret is being a bit pushy on that idea of hers, and it is getting annoying.* The ideas generated during the idea process don't belong to Tony or Margaret; they belong to all of us. Using *we* is a great reminder of that.

Rule 5: It's all good.
The final rule of (and tool for) ideation is that all ideas are good ideas.

There is certainly a time for reviewing the ideas and figuring out which of them might fly in the real world, but it is not during the ideation phase. Anyone who is shutting down ideas is threatening the creativity in the room, and to get to 100 possible solutions, you need everyone's input. As they say at IDEO, "A lot of us are smarter than any of us."

You need to do whatever you can to keep things positive while ideation rules are in force. A practical tool for keeping things positive is to write everyone's name on a piece of paper and stick it to the wall or on a white-board. Then give a "negative pen" to one person in the room (perhaps the person who is usually your devil's advocate or feeling grumpy that day) and tell them that every time someone challenges an idea, says that it has already been tried, or even squishes up their face negatively, to mark a point against that person. In our version, each mark counts as a $5 dona-tion toward our team's favorite charity. Whatever the points translate to in your version, you'll see people get competitive in openness and positiv-ity and careful about not standing out a negative member of the team.

Follow these five rules with your assembled innovation team (or teams), and you'll come up with lots of solution ideas for your "how can we" question. Getting to 100 solutions can be tough though, particularly for teams who are new to this way of thinking, so we have a few more tech-niques for you to consider as you keep innovating more solutions.

REMEMBER THAT IMITATION IS THE BEST FORM OF FLATTERY

The reality is that you don't necessarily have to reinvent the wheel to solve the problems you have identified. In fact, there is a very real possi-bility that there is a school out there who has already implemented a great solution to a similar problem.

So have a look at what other people are up to. What is already work-ing in your own school? In other schools? In other cities? Spend a bit of time searching online to see if fun things are happening that you didn't know about. Maybe put up a post on Facebook or throw out some tweets to see if people can alert you to cool things that are out there. Or tap into the collective genius of the tens of thousands of passionate educators in our tribe by joining the EC Community on Facebook or using the hashtag #educhange on Twitter.

If you reach out to other successful innovative school leaders for advice or guidance, they will most likely be thrilled. Educators are some of the most generous professionals out there. Of course, if you want to copy an idea, use your best judgment to decide whether you need to ask the creator's permission to do so, and try your best to acknowledge their work as a model for yours.

HOLD HACKATHONS

Invented by the tech industry in the late 1990s, a "hackathon" is a group of people coming together to develop a real product (originally, functioning software or websites) in a short amount of time (generally 24 to 48 hours). During a hackathon, big things can happen. The company GroupMe created a mobile messaging app that Skype purchased a year later for $85 million. Facebook invented its "Like" button at an internal hackathon.

Given that the stakes in education are higher than instant messaging and Like buttons, we are confident that a hackathon with your staff can produce some pretty great things. Bring your people together, set a design challenge with your "how can we" question, and give everyone a day or two to see what they come up with. Hackathons are fun and fast-paced, so doing them on weekends is absolutely an option, even for tired educators. Beer and pizza—though not necessary and certainly not recommended if there will be kids at the event—are excellent ways to lighten the mood and get the creative juices flowing.

RUN AN INNOVATION CHALLENGE

The "innovation challenge" concept has become more familiar over the past few years, with governments, aid organizations, and all kinds of companies now employing innovation challenges to tackle particularly complex issues. Setting one up is very simple. Choose one of your "how can we" questions and pose it to your school community. Offer some seed capital to the winning team (as little as $100 is fine) and announce that there will be an awards event where the winning team (as selected by the leadership team) will be recognized. Give people a month to come up with ideas, which they can submit online or in person at a demo day.

Tapping into people's competitive spirits is a great way to foster new ideas and demonstrate the creativity of your community.

THINK OUTSIDE THE BOX

We know. "Think outside the box" is a terrible cliché. It's what people say when they aren't getting ideas from their team and are hoping to somehow switch on the idea lightbulbs and get a flood of brilliant, left-field suggestions. But if you want people to think outside the box, you need to equip them with some skills to do that. To paraphrase Tom Dodd at Lesher Middle School, if you've got high expectations, you need to provide high support.

When someone invites a team to think outside the box, the implication is that everybody is generally thinking *inside* the box. And it's often an accurate assumption. That's because when school people try to innovate, they generally think like the educators they are. They leverage the training they have and the experiences they have amassed, which means they can be hemmed in by their existing concept of what "works" in a school setting. In other words, to get out of the box, your leadership team needs to stop thinking like educators.

Here's an example of what you have to gain. You might have heard the story of Allan Goldman and Martin Elliot, cardiac surgeons at London's Great Ormond Street Hospital for Children. It's told a lot in innovation circles and was published in the *Wall Street Journal* (Naik, 2006). Dr. Goldman and Professor Elliot performed incredibly complex operations on babies and small children. Although both were highly skilled, they confronted the truth that as they performed the many interactions and activities they had to execute during surgeries, they sometimes became clumsy and inefficient. After a particularly tough day, the two men were sacked out in front of a television in the break room. On TV was a Formula One race. As they watched, they started joking about the similarities between the Formula One pit crews and the handovers between surgeons and the intensive care doctors. The penny dropped. They decided to reach out to the McLaren and Ferrari teams to see if they couldn't collaborate with them to develop new ways of improving effectiveness in the hospital. The result was a program called Operation Pit Stop, which went on to reduce surgical and hospital care errors by more than half.

Radical collaborations and outside-the-box thinking like this can help you come up with innovative solutions you would never have thought of before. For example, a school librarian trying to reorganize the space might take a trip to IKEA and take note of how the store is set up. A teacher struggling to maintain discipline in class might take a karate lesson to see how order is kept in that environment. A leadership team at a primary school might send someone to Disney World for a fact-finding trip on immersive learning environments or sit through a Pixar movie marathon for some ideas about how to engage students through humor and storytelling. At John A. Leslie in Toronto, a succession of leadership teams brought in representatives from successful Canadian startups and learned about how these companies created and tested ideas. This collaboration was very influential in shaping the school's strategy of "Everyone a change agent."

So where can you look for some inspiration? Whom could you invite into your school for some radical collaboration? Spend some time as a leadership team innovating on this topic. And don't stress too much about finding money for this. If you look for people who are parents, who love children, or who want to support their community, you can usually find them and thus secure loads of free love and brainpower. Think back to Cornish College's origin story. The community was the source of its entrepreneurial spark and its marketing experts, designers, and million-dollar funders.

SET SOME ARTIFICIAL CONSTRAINTS

As you are innovating, chances are good that some of the ideas you come up with would require lots of work, time, and money. It's true that many of the problems schools encounter are complex and can take a long time to fix. (Remember, most of the Dream Teams were focused on their change initiatives for five to seven years.) However, it can also be helpful to play with the deadlines to see the impacts of shorter or longer time frames, more or less money, and so on. It will shift your thinking and give you additional angles to consider.

As a team, take another look at the "how can we" question you selected to work through. If you had to come up with a strategy to solve this problem in just four weeks, what could you do? What if you had to solve the problem with only $1,000 to spend?

See how this technique works for you. Keep recording your ideas. How close to 100 are you now?

IMAGINE THAT EVERYTHING IS POSSIBLE

People who work in schools tend to start as idealists and then become realists. Chances are, that's what you are too. Somewhere along the way, you began to focus more on what you can actually get done than on what you would love to get done. You came to understand that resources are limited and there is never enough money. This realistic attitude, while valuable for day-to-day survival and for sustaining energy over a long career, *is holding you back as an innovator*.

That's why, for this final push toward 100 ideas, we want you to take away all constraints. As Lee Musumeci says to her Challis staff, students, and parents, "If I were a fairy godmother and could wave my wand and literally do anything for you, what would it be?" Together with your team, imagine that time, money, and capacity isn't an issue. Now ask your "how can we" question one more time.

Remember, everyone thought JFK was mad when he stated, "We choose to go to the moon in this decade." But on July 20, 1969, Neil Armstrong set foot on the moon. It was still a very risky endeavor—so risky that President Nixon had two speeches prepared, one for a successful mission and one in the event that the astronauts never came home.

Dream big, think of some moonshots, and see what you come up with.

prioritizing, prototyping, and deciding

So, hopefully, by using a combination of the techniques we've presented in this chapter, your leadership team has come up with your 100 solutions to your "how can we" question. (We know it's likely that you are innovating on more than just one question, but for the sake of explaining the process, let's stick with just one.) What comes next? We'll tell you.

REDUCE YOUR 100 IDEAS TO YOUR TOP 2

The easiest way to do this is to allot every person on the leadership team 10 votes. Post or distribute a list of all the ideas. Team members can distribute their 10 votes any way they like: a single vote for the 10 ideas they like best, 2 votes each for their 5 favorites, or even 10 votes for an idea they really, really love. If people want to combine two related ideas into one and vote for that, we allow that, too.

The ideas you want are the ones people are excited to implement. The ones that are ambitious but possible. And of course, the ones that are honestly most likely to eliminate the root causes of the problem you've identified, if executed directly.

Significantly, now is also the time for you to give your top two ideas names so that they will start to feel real. A working title is fine, and the easiest thing to do is to fill in the gaps of "The ___ Project," or simply "Project ___." Come up with a working title for your best idea, for the "how can we" question you are working through, and jot it down somewhere. What about the 98 ideas you didn't select? Just put them to one side; you may need them later.

PROTOTYPE YOUR TOP IDEAS

By this point, after all this innovating and reflecting, your leadership team is probably starting to feel fairly confident about your chosen ideas. But the truth is you don't know if they are going to work in the real world just yet, or what other people will think of them.

So it's time to start baking some reality into these solutions. And one of the easiest ways to do this is to prototype them.

Prototyping is borrowed from the business world, where creators will build a mockup of an item to source some feedback. Fashion houses prepare samples and share them with a few stores to see how people like the fit and the material. Car manufacturers still to this day create life-size clay models of new car designs that people can sit in and experience and then talk about. In restaurants, chefs will often try out new recipes and serve them to their staff for feedback before these items make the menu.

To demonstrate the prototyping process and clarify some useful approaches, we want to take you back to one of the root causes circled on our root cause analysis tree way back in Chapter 2: "Collaboration is not valued in our school."

Say we innovated 100 solutions to the question "How can we encourage meaningful collaboration?" and then selected the two that we were most excited about. The first was "Let's let teachers renovate their classrooms to make them more collaborative." We called this one "Project Pimp My Space." The second was "Let's designate Fridays as a day for collaborative work, for both students and staff." We called it "Project Frideation."

Here is how we, as a leadership team, might prototype these ideas, using four different techniques.

Storyboard prototyping

Screenwriters and directors will storyboard specific scenes and sometimes entire scripts before a movie or TV show goes into production. If you haven't watched a video of a Disney animation team in action, you're missing out. The storyboards they create are incredibly elaborate, and they use them to tweak characters, themes, and plot lines before production gets under way.

School leadership teams can keep things a lot simpler. Creating a storyboard can mean just dividing a standard sheet of paper into six sections and drawing out what an idea looks like, started at the top left corner. Figure 7.1 shows a storyboard of our Project Frideation idea.

When presenting a prototype like this, ask for feedback in the form of "I like/I wish" statements. For example, "I *like* that we are being radical and taking the entire Friday off, but I *wish* we had planned for more interaction between teachers and students on Fridays."

Try this yourself. Draw up a storyboard for one of your ideas and show it to some people. Find out what they like about it and what they wish you could do better.

Persona prototyping

Persona prototyping involves explaining the effect your idea will have on the people it is intended to affect. You create a fictional representative of one such person, who, depending on your team's specific focus, might be a staff member, a student, a parent, and so on. Then you draw a quick cartoon of this persona, describe his or her current situation, and describe how the solution will change that situation for the better. Once people have read through the one-page prototype, ask for additional feedback in the "I like/I wish" format.

In Figure 7.2, you'll find a persona protype for Project Frideation, built around a teacher we call "Lonely Leonard." Personas are a quick and fun way to get feedback. Just be careful with the names and drawings. You don't want to upset or offend sensitive members of your staff.

Miniature prototyping

Another quick way to get feedback on your team's ideas is to build a little model of it. Usually you won't have to look far in your school to find some things to help you build your prototype. Search out some Lego pieces, pipe cleaners, toilet paper rolls, and cardboard and quickly piece together a model for people to take a look at. Get their feedback in the form of "I like/I wish."

Figure 7.1

Storyboard Prototype

The problem is that we don't value collaboration at our school.

Every Friday, regular classes are canceled. Students and staff still come to school.

Students and staff all work in the Main Hall. Students work in multiyear groups at some tables; staff work at others.

Students work on self-directed enterprises, creating small businesses that solve problems for people in their community.

Teachers work in teams to plan units, assess work, and learn from one another. They review their past week of teaching and get ready for the next week together.

Once a month, teams of students and staff are profiled at a school assembly. They share their successful methods of working collaboratively.

Figure 7.2

Persona Prototype

Lonely Leonard

The Situation. Leonard is a first-year teacher at Lonewolf Lane Middle School. He's struggling to plan interesting lessons for his 7th grade science students, and he is not quite sure how to assess them against benchmarks.

Leonard asked the other 7th grade science teacher for some help, but she said she was too busy.

Leonard is not sure how he is going to get through the year, let alone the rest of his working life in this profession.

The Solution. Frideation. Every Friday regular classes are canceled. Instead, students work in collaborative teams on self-directed student enterprises, applying and developing 21C skills to solve real-world problems. At the same time, teachers have the day to work in teams to learn together, plan units, and assess work collaboratively.

Both teachers and students work in the Main Hall so that students are being supervised and so that ways of working collaboratively are being modeled.

We once worked with a group of children who were passionate about improving the diets of their fellow students. They came up with "Breakfast Bar" (with a logo inspired by the television show *Breaking Bad*), which was a student-led café that would compete with McDonald's and Subway franchises across the road. They built two Lego prototypes, one of which showed where the Breakfast Bar would be located; this is the one they showed to school leadership to gain approval for their desired café site. With this Lego prototype, the leadership team was able to physically move different parts of the café around to different places to ensure a better flow of students around the school, particularly during the busy time as kids were arriving. Their second Lego prototype was for their peers, and it showed the different kinds of products that the Breakfast Bar would sell. When unveiling the prototype, the student innovators issued pretend money and asked their classmates to choose which items they would buy. The team was then able to determine which products they would launch with. As an interesting side note, this student-led café was so successful that it ended up winning the contract for the school canteen, beating the company that had been doing this work for the previous decade!

Life-size model prototyping

Still another prototyping option is to create a life-size model of your idea, just like the carmakers do with their clay creations.

Let's say we want to prototype Project Pimp My Space, attaching it to a learning approach focused on cross-grade student collaboration on projects. One lunchtime, we might set up a class in the new manner we are proposing. Then we would invite a few teachers and students to come in and walk around while we explained how the class would work.

We know that teachers don't have a lot of patience for role-plays, but if you do have the guts to use this prototyping tool, you can get some great feedback very quickly, and you might even move furniture around immediately based on the feedback you receive.

NOW, MAKE A DECISION

So keeping with our example of "How can we better prepare our students for a positive future?" we have gone from creating at least 100 ideas to solve one of the root causes we are focusing on, down to our favorite two that we prototyped: Project Frideation and Project Pimp My Space. We received some feedback on our ideas and have made some changes. Now how do we decide which one we want to actually launch in the school? Just the one we feel better about? The one that people voted most often for?

Yes, this information can help us get to a decision, but this is also a great time to look to research data and see what might happen to student achievement if we pursued one of these ideas.

Let's consider Project Pimp My Space first and use various online tools to investigate the effect sizes of the interventions this idea involves. It turns out that "classroom reorganization," for example, has an effect size of .01. Not a great start. Next, we'll use the organization Social Ventures Australia's (www.socialventures.com.au) online tool for estimating the monthly learning progress associated with specific interventions. It tells us that "physical changes in a classroom" translates into zero months of learning progress. This is a bummer. The data are not looking great for Project Pimp My Space. So, should we kill off this idea?

Well, not so fast. We have already received some good feedback with our prototype. As a team, we are really liking it as well; it came through our filtering process from 100 down to 2. Maybe there is someone on our team who believes strongly in the positive outcomes of changing our physical environment and is willing to find some evidence-based strategies that we may be able to try. Maybe we are going for outcomes that are not usually captured by the types of studies we decided to look at. Maybe there are some great new things that the academics haven't got around to including in their studies just yet. Or maybe we have a confidence that our new approach is going to be a positive revolution, and that we (and maybe some academics one day) will be able to prove that a new approach to space can have brilliant outcomes for kids. Because the reality is that academics need innovators like us. We come up with the new approaches that they can study and publish papers about a few years later!

There are enough "maybes" here for us not to throw out the idea entirely. While the research is important, and we should do a bit more of it ourselves before we launch into the idea, we might still think it is worth a trial. But for now, based on positive feedback from a bunch of people and a strong evidence base (we searched for "collective efficacy," and the effect size was awesome!), we may choose to go ahead with Project Frideation instead.

Good luck prototyping your best ideas, digging into the research, and then deciding which ones you want to bring into the school. You are getting to the pointy end of the Change Leader Journey now, having devoted significant effort to finding focus, preparing people for change, and building out cultures that have helped you innovate some great solutions. And while we have encouraged your leadership team to innovate a bunch of solutions, what we are really hoping is that you foster creativity across your community to source ideas from them. In most cases, the best ideas will emerge from your staff, students, and parents, rather than from the leadership team alone.

When the process of innovating approaches its natural end, you will still have a lot of work to do to turn these ideas into reality and embed them in the school. We'll sink our teeth into that in Chapter 8.

8
SOLUTIONS

How can we turn our innovative ideas into real change?

Ray Trotter had always been a pretty good handyman. As a former foot-baller, cricketer, and sports coach, he was not afraid to break a sweat to get a job done. For a few years, his leadership team at Wooranna Park Primary School had been working to make the school as engaging as possible for all students. This approach meant making a dramatic strategic shift from the old way of prioritizing the gifted and talented programs.

Ray and the team had a new idea. They were going to make a time machine for the grade 1 students. They had a little bit of money to invest, but not a lot. There were a few parents willing to lend some time and a teacher who was very adept with a saw and a hammer who would also be a big help. Drawings were quickly made, and after a few trips to the hard-ware store, work began in earnest over the holiday break.

Two weeks later, the time machine was finished. It had enough room for four kids to step inside. There were lights that lit up, levers to be pulled, and sound effects. The best part, though—the part that had taken the most time to figure out but that the kids were going to *love*—was that the time machine moved. It spun around in circles when the students indicated they wanted to be transported to a different moment in history.

The mantra of Wooranna Park being "as exciting as Disneyland" had been around for a few years by then, but the members of the leadership team felt that they had outdone themselves with this one. How many grade 1 classes in Melbourne, or in the world for that matter, had time machines? They tested it out a few times to make sure it was safe, with fire extinguishers handy in case the motor that spun the thing decided to be uncooperative, but everything worked just fine.

The team delighted as they saw the grade 1s come into the class on their first day after break. The looks on the children's faces when they saw the time machine said it all: *School was in, and school was awesome.*

There was one big problem though. As the time machine spun, it made the students feel sick. Determined to see his machine succeed, Ray hopped on himself and spent a few minutes whirring around before he had to stop the motor and get off, his legs wobbly and his stomach doing circles. While their time machine was as engaging as a Disneyland ride, as a learning tool that teachers could use consistently, it just wasn't going to work.

Since then, the leadership team at Wooranna Park has gone on to build many more incredible spaces in the school, like the Enigma Centre, the Space Ship, the Giant Dragon, and the Castle. All of these make for brilliant learning approaches to accompany classroom designs. But the failure of his time machine still irritates Ray, and if he could truly go back in time, it would be to do this learning space differently.

setting the stage for success

The reality is that not every idea your leadership team and wider school community come up with is going to work. If you are going to push for great creativity and innovation, that's something you'll just need to accept. But there are certainly things that you can do at this stage to lay a better foundation for success, and the first thing is to acknowledge that educators have a certain proclivity that can hold them back. Educators are in love with pilots. Not the kind of pilots who stroll through airports looking dashing in their blazers, but the long, drawn-out, complex pilot projects that schools always seem to be implementing.

So the second thing you can do is ask, "What if we did fewer of these long, drawn-out pilots and more quick tests to figure out if our idea is a good and workable solution?"

For a school example, let's jump back into one of the things that Dave and his leadership team did at Halls Creek when they were at this step on the Change Leader Journey.

Brain Food

Dave Faulkner
Halls Creek, Western Australia, 2008

Behavior was a huge problem at Halls Creek.

As a leadership team, we had explored all the possible reasons why the students were being so disruptive, and the root cause we decided to focus on was an unconventional one. We didn't have a functioning school cafeteria, and at lunchtime, the kids were sneaking out of the building and across the road to buy junk food. Even 6-year-olds were getting through a liter of Coca-Cola and greasy bags of fries in the middle of the school day. As a result (we hypothesized), afternoons were absolute mayhem. Teachers were losing control of their sugar- and caffeine-amped charges, and Halls Creek was losing teachers who just couldn't cope.

When we started innovating, one of our teachers came up with the idea of giving the kids healthy food at school for breakfast and lunch. She was absolutely adamant that this would make a real difference.

Given that we were willing to try anything by this point, the idea got the thumbs-up.

Now the old way of doing this would have been to set up a big expensive pilot program to improve our school cafeteria offerings. It would have taken a month or two to draft a proposal, a year or so to get the pilot funding into the central office budget, and hundreds of thousands of dollars to make the pilot program happen. In our part of the country, these kinds of pilots were executed by people who didn't come up with the ideas and had limited buy-in. They would write a big report that almost nobody would read, and in all likelihood, nothing would ever change. If we were lucky, being as remote as we were, Halls Creek would have an improved cafeteria and a healthy food program in two years.

Two years. *If* we were lucky. Two whole years of continuing behavior issues and a revolving door of new teachers unable to handle the challenge.

It was madness to wait two years, particularly when we didn't even know if a healthy breakfast and lunch would have any effect on our behavior situation. So instead, we set up a simple little experiment. We paid a local café to make a healthy breakfast and a healthy lunch for one class of students (the children with the worst behavior levels). We didn't even tell our central office, because we managed to direct a little bit of budget in the direction of this new idea.

The test lasted two weeks. Over that period, we tracked the number of behavior incidents in our test class. They dropped by 40 percent.

No, we hadn't solved our behavior problem entirely, but we always knew the entire answer was never going to be as simple as a few sandwiches. And we had made progress—enough to justify "baking in" this approach as one of our behavior initiatives moving forward. We went on to roll it out strategically to different parts of the school.

TEST YOUR IDEA—QUICKLY AND CHEAPLY

Now direct your attention back to your team's favorite idea (remembering, of course, that you came up with a few solutions to a few different root causes that your team is tackling). You have identified this idea as a potential solution to one of your problems.

We encourage you to test it, quickly and cheaply, just as Dave and the Halls Creek team did with their healthy-breakfast-and-lunch idea. It's a great way to figure out if an idea's truly worth pursuing—much better, we think, than a long, slow, expensive pilot program.

Obviously, when you are testing an idea with kids, you need to keep the following in mind:

1. The kids must be safe, and you must ensure that the test will not seriously affect them or their learning in a negative way.

2. Don't get people's hopes up too much. You can keep expectations low by testing your idea quietly, without heralding the results you're expecting or implying that this is the way things are going to be from now on.

3. If you can, go into the test with an estimation of what the data or effect size of your idea will be. We say, "if you can," because while there are loads of great research out there, each context calls for different ideas, and you can't always move forward by looking back.

4. Related to the previous point, set some clear success criteria. For example, Dave's team at Halls Creek might have said that anything less than a 10 percent reduction in behavior incidents was not significant enough to justify the program investment, and anything more than a 30 percent reduction was a clear sign of effectiveness.

ACCEPT THAT SOMETIMES IT DOESN'T WORK OUT

If your leadership team is committed to using these small tests to determine whether the ideas being developed are effective, everyone needs to keep one additional and very important point in mind: the tests might fail. In the cold, hard light of day, your idea might come up short.

If your test ends up being a failure based on the criteria you set, you really have two options. You can pivot, whereby you try to innovate another idea or test one of the other 99 ideas produced during your ideation time. Or you can persevere, based on the belief that with a few changes based on the feedback you received in the test, the idea is still worth going after. Doing neither of these, however, and pushing ahead with a flawed concept is folly.

In innovation circles, the ideas that you have real reservations about but insist on pursuing anyway are commonly known as "bad boyfriend ideas." The bad boyfriend is the leather jacket–wearing, motorbike-riding type who never buys gifts, is always cheating on his partner, and basically has no positive prospects for the future. You think that if you love him more, one day he will change and be everything you hope for. Chances are, that day will never come. He is a bad boyfriend, and although it might hurt to finally let him go, it'd be better for you in the long run. If nothing else, you would be free to pursue someone new.

At Challis Community Primary School, the leadership team told us they regularly own up to their failures, but over the years, the failures have become smaller as they have become better at testing ideas. At Lesher Middle School, the leadership team shared failures by writing about them in weekly newsletters sent out to parents. At Manurewa Intermediate School, the team was filled with persevering types who took the data generated from failed tests and kept revising ideas until they worked—even if those ideas ended up totally different from what was first proposed!

As a team of change leaders, you will often get excited by ideas that you or your staff come up with. You may innovate a new solution on a Tuesday and then spend the next two days telling everyone about how amazing it is going to be. Maybe by Thursday, though, you have tired of the idea and are ready to quietly throw it into the trash. If you do, great. Better a few days of your time wasted than a few years!

DON'T BE AFRAID TO REALIGN PRIORITIES

Another important thing to consider at this step in the process is that you may need to kill off some of the existing programs or ideas in the school as you bring new ones on board. At Bayview, the leadership team shut down several initiatives that were misaligned with the new direction and too resource-dependent. This advice applies to new initiatives as well. The team at Bayview admitted, "Sometimes our promises were a little too big. When this was the case, we would apologize and tell everyone that we got excited, overcommitted, and got it wrong."

The team at John Polanyi Collegiate Institute once killed off a new idea not because they thought it was a bad idea but because they realized they hadn't yet laid the necessary groundwork. Eager to provide powerful and future-focused learning opportunities for their students, they announced they were putting a freeze on buying textbooks and would instead invest heavily in technology, particularly in tablets. There was an outcry from parents, and before long, it became clear that parents were not ready for such a bold move. The leadership team didn't fight back and insist that their idea was the right call; they sucked up their egos and acknowledged the mistake. Rather than saying, "We know better, so we're doing it anyway," they stated, "If you want books for your kids, we will get the books."

If people think your idea stinks, it doesn't matter how many nice ribbons you tie around it trying to convince them it is great; they still think it stinks, and you need to have the courage to get rid of it and try something else. Or to put it another way, in the words of brand strategy consultant Stephen Denny, "If dogs don't like your dog food, the packaging doesn't matter."

turning an idea into an initiative

So let's say you have pivoted a few times and finally landed on an idea that has passed the tests you set up. You're reasonably sure it's the solution you need. Now is when you need to embed it in the school and turn it from a test into a real product or program—from an idea to an initiative that you will roll out.

What do you do now?

TEST THE MARKET

The first thing you need is buy-in for your solution, and one of the easiest ways to get it is for your leadership team to get really good at "pitching it."

This concept comes from the world of entrepreneurship. You might be familiar with it thanks to television shows like *Shark Tank* or *Dragon's Den*. Earlier in the book we talked about the techniques that you can use to engage your community with the idea of embracing a change: telling stories and presenting numbers to make a compelling case for it. The pitch you need to build now is slightly different. It must quickly and powerfully present your idea and encourage people in your school to get on board. Every member of your leadership team needs to get good at pitching, because you all will have to draw on this skill in a load of different contexts—from parent–teacher nights to visits from your superintendent to staff meetings, school assemblies, and even conversations in the corridor—and you'll likely need to keep pitching over the life of the initiative.

A pitch is a tool for seeing if an idea will get up or not. Even though you are yet to launch the project in your school, you can still pitch it to see if the appetite that you think exists actually does. Entrepreneurs and innovators use similar techniques all the time. Fashion designers present new lines each season, showing designs they are planning to offer. Often when we, as people not in the fashion industry, see clips of these shows, we wonder, "Who on earth would wear that?" Well, the reality is, maybe no one. Usually the models on the catwalk are wearing the only version of each garment in existence. The buyers place orders just for what they want, and factories standing at the ready whip into production. Crowdfunding follows the same principle. Someone comes up with an idea they think is great, they record a fun video pitch to share it with the world, and they see how many people buy their product through pre-orders. When they see there's sufficient interest, they bring the product to market at scale.

REFINE YOUR PITCH WITH THE NINE Cs

So here are our tips to help you create and perfect a powerful and compelling pitch that will encourage people to buy into the solution that your leadership team has landed on. We call them the Nine Cs.

Complete

The first thing you need to decide when you begin to build your pitch is what information it must include.

A great way to do this is to imagine that you're in an elevator. Just before the doors close, Bill Gates walks in and presses the button for the ground floor. You have 60 seconds to sell him on your great idea before the elevator reaches the ground floor and he and his billions walk out of your life forever. What would you say? You couldn't tell him everything, but you would try to include the most important parts to give him the fullest possible picture.

What you have to do here is strip away the unnecessary so the necessary can be heard. When you are pitching a new idea to staff, students, parents, funders, or your fellow leaders, make sure that the simple, important information is included, and be sure to leave out the parts that are not necessary to share at that particular moment.

Concise

We said just now that you had 60 seconds to sell elevator-riding Bill Gates on your idea, and neither that time frame nor that setting was random. Entrepreneurs often refer to their pitches as "elevator pitches." The implication is that you need to be able to get all the important information across in less than 60 seconds. Of course, you can accordion this out when you have a little more time, but 60 seconds is the benchmark. The reason that we keep them so short is that people are busy, so we need to get a sense of their engagement with the idea quickly; nobody has time for a one-hour presentation.

And to be honest, being that concise is not easy.

Here's how Mark Twain once summed up the challenge of concise communication: "My dear, I didn't have time to write you a short letter, so I wrote a long one instead." And, as E. F. Schumacher, author of the 1973 economics classic *Small Is Beautiful*, once said, "Any intelligent fool can make things bigger, more complex, and more violent. It takes a touch of genius—and a lot of courage—to move in the opposite direction."

But our favorite anecdote on the power of concise language comes from a story that is attributed to Hemingway. As the legend goes, a group of writers placed a bet to see who could write the most powerful story in 10 words or less. Hemingway was said to have waited for the pot to be passed around, watching it fill with money. Then he wrote on a napkin, "For sale: baby shoes, never worn." He drank free for the rest of the month.

When you are pitching your ideas, don't take an eternity; be as concise and powerful as you can.

Clear

Educators are, by and large, terrible at keeping things simple. We attend PD on PBL so we can try to raise the SATs of our ESL students with ADD. And while it makes us feel pretty cool when we understand all of these TLAs (three-letter acronyms—did you know that one?), we usually lose everyone else in the room who doesn't get them.

When pitching your idea, don't try to win credibility points by using big words. Focus instead on making sure your message is heard and understood. Acronyms, buzz words, and insider language are distracting and dilute the clarity of your message, so get rid of them. Remember, this is *a good idea* you're presenting. When it's easy for everyone to understand that it's a good idea and why it's a good idea, more of them will get on board.

Compelling

Again, this a reminder that tapping into people's emotions will inspire them to move. If they are feeling sad or angry about a problem, you can use that when crafting your pitch, especially when you can present a solution that you really think will work to solve that problem.

We witnessed a great example of this approach when we saw a leadership team from a very well-to-do Catholic school pitching a new transition program to their teachers. They started by painting a picture of a new 13-year-old boy at the school who was finding it really difficult to fit in. Once they had built up a powerful image of a sad and lonely young student, they asked the teachers to imagine that this boy was their own son. Then they asked for support for their idea. If that team could make transition compelling, we are confident that you will be able to stir the emotions with the challenges you are trying to solve!

As you refine your pitch, see if people in your audience are leaning in. Are you giving them goosebumps of inspiration when you talk? Do they seem genuinely interested in your solution? Do you have a powerful line to hook them with? Are you telling a compelling story? You've got to move people when you are pitching, because if you can't, they won't buy what you are selling.

Credible

The unfortunate reality is that people will begin judging you from the moment you begin your pitch—and some, even before. So as quickly as you can, you need to establish the credibility necessary to ground your case. A handful of ways to do this are to

- Bring data to back up your claims.
- Share the experience you bring that will help to make your solution successful.
- Really believe what you're saying (if you don't, adjust your pitch until you do).
- Come across as confident (if you don't, practice until you do).

You communicate credibility by how well you pitch and how convincing you can be. It will even come across via your dress and bearing and whether you appear to be a leadership team capable of making the initiative a success. The ways in which your team is deployed can make a real difference here. On your team, you are likely to have a blend of *estimators* (people who like to tell stories to help paint a picture and have a habit of exaggerating things or glossing over specifics) and *exactors* (those who aren't as good at storytelling and want to make sure that the exact facts are used). When working as a team to fine-tune a pitch, you want to balance the contributions of the estimators, who can make a pitch engaging, and the exactors, who can fact-check it to make sure you don't get caught out slinging "alternative facts."

Overall, making sure your pitch is credible means doing everything you can to ensure that the individuals you are pitching to are looking at you and thinking, *Here is a big problem, and I am really glad that this particular leadership team is trying to tackle it.*

Contextualized

Rather than rolling out the same sales pitch to everyone in every situation, you need to ensure that your pitch makes absolute sense to the different groups of people you will be sharing it with. This means that if you are pitching an idea to parents, target your language, ideas, and description of the initiative's benefits to them. If it is to students, make sure it is engaging to them. If it is to teachers, work to connect it to their professional passions and be sure it will come across as achievable given all the other responsibilities they must attend to within the classroom.

For an example of a pitch that was effectively contextualized, we turn again to the 21st Century Parenting program, mentioned in Chapter 5. The leadership team was able to sell students on a really exciting update to the school's learning style, telling them about the coding classes, robotics, and entrepreneurship courses that would be launched the next term. Teachers got a different pitch—an aspirational and inspirational one that focused on adapting education to meet evolving needs. It included case studies of some of the world's most forward-thinking schools. The team's pitch to parents was about carefully bringing them along in the journey and encouraging them to see future-focused learning as critical for their children's security, success, and happiness.

As a team, work hard to hone your messages for all the contexts you foresee. What other audiences do you have? What other factors will resonate most with them? When you can, test these contextualized presentations with representatives of the different groups that you will be pitching to.

Consistent

While you do need a great pitch that is easily contextualized, you also need one that's consistently effective. Everyone in your leadership team should be able to pitch the strategy well. You are all representing it, and you all must be able to seize the opportunities that arise to evangelize for it.

With this in mind, ensure that different members of the team are getting opportunities to pitch the idea so all of you will be "game-fit" as pitchers.

Conversational

You know that feeling you get when you're being sold a used car or approached by a charity worker on the street seeking a monthly donation? That "get me out of here, work up an excuse" feeling? This is what you can trigger when you speak *at* an audience rather than with them.

Even though you only have 60 seconds to make your pitch (if you are aiming for the gold standard), you want to be as conversational as possible when you are trying to engage people with your idea. A great trick to turn a pitch into something that feels more like a conversation is to ask questions. Did they realize that the numbers were this? Do they remember what math class was like when they were in school? Do they have a real sense of how quickly education is changing? You get the idea.

Visualization prompts work too. We saw a great example of it in a school where the leadership team was pitching a new program to provide enhanced support to the most disengaged children. They asked their teachers to picture a great class that they were running, and then to picture one student interrupting the class and undermining the great flow. With this student in mind, they were able to make a case that this new program would improve behavior in classrooms and also be really beneficial for the disengaged student.

A conversational pitch is one that connects you to the audience. You want it to feel more like a two-way chat than a one-way sell.

Close

This is the verb *close* we're talking about here. It's entrepreneur-speak for asking for something, be it a deal, money, permission, or insights. How you conclude a pitch is probably the most important part of the 60 seconds, because it's where you make "the ask." Every pitch should have a clear ask.

Maybe you need funding from your superintendent. Maybe you need five teachers to come along to a professional development session that afternoon. Or maybe you need a show of hands from the students to see if they are interested in your idea. Whatever you need, make the ask at the end of your pitch as clear as possible.

the early days of an idea

The first nonprofit Aaron ever launched was called Spark, and it existed to help startup entrepreneurs in very poor communities turn very small ideas into big powerful projects that could help many people. It was called Spark because ideas the organization was seeking out were only tiny sparks of possibility. A spark can fizzle out quickly. It can be extinguished by a raindrop or blown away in the wind. But if a spark is nurtured, protected from the elements, and given some fuel to burn, it might just turn into a mighty flame.

Ideas during the early stages of change are like these sparks. They need some love to turn into a flame. What are the best and most practical ways to do this in a school setting?

THINK BIG AND ACT SMALL

Even now, after you have prototyped and tested the idea, it is still wise to start small. For example, if your new initiative is to bring in technology devices, consider bringing them in with only 30 students initially, tracking those students for a month to see how the initiative goes, and learning from this.

Imagine you have a nice lamp in the room where your team gathers to work. The lamp is a bit old and out-of-date, and it flickers now. It also uses a lot of electricity, so it costs a lot to run. You decide it's time for a new lamp. However, you still need to keep the tricky lamp going for a while longer, because if you throw it out, everyone will be plunged into darkness. So while the old lamp burns, a few people on the team start to research the alternatives that are in the market, and before long, they narrow down the selection to one they really like. It is efficient to run, emits a lovely light, and basically is the bee's knees of lamps. They are sure everyone is going to love it. The thing is, this lamp is a little complex to assemble and calibrate. When the new lamp arrives, everyone can all cheer and get very excited, but you want to keep an eye on it for a little while longer, letting it operate alongside the old lamp. You only begin to dim the old light as you become more confident in the new one, adjusting it to do everything it is capable of doing.

Then there will come a time when you're all convinced the new lamp is perfect. At that point, you can decide whether to keep the old lamp on, because it still works well sometimes, or you can retire it to the cupboard, bringing it out occasionally to remember what it was like and how you used to do things.

Just like with the new light, start small as you implement your ideas, and then as they prove to be successful, roll them out across the school.

KEEP IMPROVING

The chances are your idea won't be perfect right from the get-go. As you roll it out across the school, be sure to track how it is going with key metrics as well as anecdotal insights from the people who are using it. Think of this like the software updates that you do on your smartphone, where the developers are continually tweaking and improving the model. In the early days of these solutions being rolled out across the school, these insights should be regularly collected and tweaks made often. As it improves, you can push this out to half-yearly or annual reviews.

GIVE PEOPLE THE TOOLS

Because your team has been so involved with creating the idea, it will make a lot of sense to you, and if you were to be running it yourselves, you would most likely feel confident. However, other members of the staff, while they have likely had some exposure to the concept, will not be as comfortable with it as you. So before you implement it formally in the school, make sure people have the skills and approaches they need to be successful. As instructional leaders, you will have an insight into the ways that your staff learn best, but you should consider classroom observations, the creation of videos, training packs, and orientation programs. The more supported your staff feel to execute these ideas as they were intended, the more comfortable they will feel doing so in the school.

BE EXPLICIT

All of the leadership teams we studied used the same key strategy at this part of their change journey. They made themselves very clear and raised the expectations that they had of everyone to implement the ideas professionally and powerfully.

For the change to succeed, they needed everyone to grow a few inches, to lean in and take control where needed, and to expect more of themselves and one another. With these higher expectations came greater accountability—another point that was clearly made.

At Manurewa Intermediate, the leadership team changed the school motto from "Be honest" to the mantra "All the time, every time, all of us, everywhere." It was posted all over the school and printed on bracelets worn by every staff member. Eventually, this commitment to all-in, communitywide investment fueled Manurewa's new vision: "Adventurous risk takers, persistent focused achievers."

At Lesher, the leadership team articulated higher expectations with the words *character* and *competence*—qualities demanded of every staff member. Anyone who fell short in either or both of these areas received focused and intensive training and support from the leadership team. In most cases, this intervention helped staff members make dramatic improvement; in some cases, it led staff members to depart, realizing that Lesher was no longer the right fit for them.

As a team you should feel confident in the ideas. They were created with powerful insights from your community and they have survived testing. Turning them into action is exciting, and expecting the best of your people will accelerate their implementation even more.

what the dream teams did

By this point, you have been journeying with the different schools in this book through several key stages. You have learned about the passions of their leadership teams. You read about their strategies for listening to their communities and how they determined their key areas for change and built cultures of leaders and learners who could solve the problems they were up against. Now is where we take a look at what they actually did.

CHALLIS COMMUNITY PRIMARY SCHOOL

"We changed our definition of who our students were."
Primary schools in Australia generally engage with their incoming cohort of students only briefly, perhaps with a transition day or two that is organized with the feeder kindergartens.

The team at Challis decided to go well beyond this.

In Armadale, if you are a child in the catchment area of Challis, the first time you meet a member of the Challis team will be when you are 6 weeks old. That's right. Just as parents are coming to terms with the basics of feeding, sleeping, diaper changes, and bathing, the Challis team is working with them to set their child on a path to be school-ready by age 6 and performing at or beyond age level. This service is holistic and constant, with parents accessing support programs, health care, and engaging learning activities for children ranging from babyhood through the preschool years.

The Challis team's second innovation was a new approach to instruction. Guided by a no-excuses mentality, they worked to improve teaching by embracing explicit teaching, with a particular focus on synthetic phonics. Because this was a direction well supported by data and effect sizes, they were able to push back when other trends came knocking—among them, play-based learning, which they chose to stay away from. These approaches to learning became the Challis way, and all teachers are now expected to align with them.

And the final innovation, which we have touched on already, is the Challis approach to distributed leadership, their "18 leaders" in particular. To support it, they freed up a deputy principal salary, and this creative use of staffing has paid dividends for their leadership culture and the learning environment. Building clear processes for how these 18 leaders engage with one another and bring consistent improvements has been paramount to the school's success, ensuring the changes will endure well beyond the charismatic influence of one or two exceptional individuals.

JOHN A. LESLIE MIDDLE SCHOOL

"We created a learning environment where everyone was a changemaker."

The approach of "everyone a changemaker" was not a one-off project or a stage that the school went through. It has come to fundamentally define how learning happens at John A. Leslie, how problems are solved, and the organizational culture.

The shift took time, and a key element was the entrepreneurship training conducted with all students, in partnership with successful Canadian startups. Initially this training was done in isolation, as an add-on to existing pedagogy; later it came to underlie all learning. Before long, Greg McLeod told us, "Grade 1s were self-assessing as hackers and hustlers, and grade 2s were providing demonstrations of their work to leadership. We pivoted to making this a whole-school approach when we realized how excited the students were about these ideas." This shift saw their students competing in and often winning global entrepreneurship competitions, engaging with organizations like the United Nations, and closer to home, working to solve local community and environmental challenges.

The schoolwide embrace of changemaking led John. A. Leslie to replace the existing computer lab with mobile technology, tablet computers, and effective wi-fi. It became a "bring your own device" school, a move that was widely supported by parents and the regional office.

JEREMIAH E. BURKE HIGH SCHOOL

"We shifted to educating the whole child—acknowledging where they are now and believing in where they can go."

Given a strong mandate under the district's turnaround policy, the Burke's reinvigorated leadership team completely redesigned the learning approach in the school. Their goal was to foster environments and approaches that would engage students who were coming from challenging contexts and account for the social and emotional realities that they were experiencing. As Artis Street, a mathematics leader at the Burke said, "How can you expect a kid to engage in class when he has seen someone murdered on the street the night before?"

The whole child became the center of every interaction with students, and all staff members were supported to improve their cultural proficiency and work within a greater understanding of how poverty and trauma affect learning. Punitive reactions to disruptive students were entirely replaced by positive support and a deep and authentic desire from all staff to stop, listen, and understand. Leaders who had held the unenviable role of disciplinarians were retrained or replaced by engagement officers.

College readiness, previously a focus for just 11th and 12th graders and their teachers, became a major focus for all students and staff. Guidance counselors were retrained or replaced. Grade point averages receded in importance as the new "student development counselors" began helping students dream up and then pursue future success on their terms. Cognizant that significant ground had to be covered if the Burke students were to catch up to their age-level expectations, the school day was extended by a full 90 minutes to provide more time for learning and engagement.

Finally, to support parent and community buy-in with the new approaches at the Burke, staff members started taking time during the summer holidays to knock on the doors of all of the roughly 120 incoming freshmen. They met the students and their parents and guardians, they listened, they built a fuller picture of each child, and they were thus better prepared to support these students' transition to high school. The Burke also launched night classes for parents, providing learning on a wide range of educational opportunities as well as more consistent engagement with the school's learning approach and information about what parents could be doing at home to support it.

The system leaders expected a major change when they pushed the Burke into "turnaround status." They got it.

MANUREWA INTERMEDIATE SCHOOL

"We became a school that the community is proud of, and they see us as relevant."

If you travel to New Zealand, you will quickly notice how deeply Maori and Pacific Island culture is embedded in the country. From the world-famous All Blacks performing their haka before rugby games, to the common use of Maori language on public signs, traditional culture is a part of the community and the way of life.

The leadership team of Manurewa drew on this and directed significant energy toward building a sense of tribal belonging in each of their four *whanaus,* a Maori word for "family." Approach any student at the school and you will be able to tell which whanau he or she belongs to simply by checking the color of the rubber bracelet that almost everyone—students and teachers—chooses to wear. Many never take their bracelet off. There's an ongoing competition throughout the year with whanaus collecting points for attendance, test results, behavior, and acts of innovation or initiative. And the prizes for these competitions? Nothing other than pride. Particularly influential teachers are selected to be "passionators," pillars of inspiration for the students in each whanau. At school singing every Friday, the passionators lead whole-whanau chants, which reach a fever pitch. For anyone who's never seen a Maori haka, it's quite a sight.

The leaders at Manurewa believe in importing successful innovations in other schools and collaborating with successful partners. One example of this was when they brought in Dr. Angus Macfarlane, an expert in culturally responsive education and a man of Maori descent. On his advice, and without lessening their encouragement of whole-school pride, the school moved to create culturally appropriate spaces for Maori children and children from specific Pacific Island contexts. The parents and the community were brought into this design work, and over time, the school become a meeting place and a place of pride during open school and community days.

The leadership team also leaned on the philosophies of Italy's Reggio Emilia, with a particular focus on the environment of the school. Once, Manurewa was the picture of disrepair, with badly damaged classrooms and graffiti everywhere. At one point, it had the highest vandalism bill of any school in New Zealand. Even though countryman John Hattie's research found that a school's physical space had a low effect size on learning (2009), Manurewa's leadership team invested heavily in cleaning up the school, landscaping common areas, building engaging learning environments, and where possible, commissioning new structures. A skateboard park that was open to the community was built, with the students appointed as its caretakers. The leadership team decided that a great school should look great as well.

And finally, but most important from an instructional leadership perspective, Manurewa raised its academic expectations dramatically. In line with the mantra "All the time, every time, all of us, everywhere," each member of the learning community was now expected to perform at the highest levels. Throughout the school year, students who were falling short received specific support for improvement. Teachers who were underperforming received targeted and intensive support of their own. After appropriate assistance and management, if they were still coming up short, they were let go.

The leadership team of Manurewa was not willing to build an adequate school in a challenging community. They decided not to stop until they were one of the most outstanding schools in the country.

CORNISH COLLEGE

"We re-created the school that our community wanted."

The inspiring story of a group of parents rallying to buy a school and keep it alive is a unique one. As "customers," they effectively bought the school, which gave them the freedom to re-create it to align with the hopes and goals that they had for their children's future and for the generations of students who would follow.

Interestingly, Cornish College's leadership team kept the learning approaches exactly as they were. The campus was blessed with a huge plot of land, including grazing fields, bushland, and wetlands that were overflowing with biodiversity. This land had always been at the core of learning, supporting fascinating links to sustainability and global citizenship. Accepting that as a leadership team composed of parents, they were not qualified or experienced educators themselves, they gave a full vote of confidence for the teaching team to continue with the existing pedagogy that had made the school so compelling to parents and students to begin with.

Based on the feedback they had received from the community, the Cornish team reduced the school's fees, providing savings to existing parents and attracting new ones who saw the school as a newly affordable and accessible option for their children. The how of the fee reduction was interesting. To offset it, the leadership team decided to deprioritize major infrastructure expenses that were not directly linked to learning. Large and pricey projects like a multipurpose school hall and performing arts center were canned, and this produced a much healthier set of financials.

Cornish also underwent further expansion that took it from a grades 7–12 school to a K–12 one. The leaders reasoned that more families would be attracted to a school that kids could attend from kindergarten all the way to university. It brought more students into what had been under-populated classrooms . . . and, of course, brought in more tuition dollars.

Cornish's initial level of parent engagement was not a flash in the pan. Parents and teachers continued to work together closely to secure the school's future, and learning opportunities were bolstered by parents willing to volunteer their time, knowledge, and sweat to make the school a success. They had all authored the plan together. They even came up with the name together. The result was a feeling of widespread ownership that most schools could only dream of. Out of the ashes of a failed model, Cornish College was born, and it has gone on to be an absolute success.

BAYVIEW SECONDARY COLLEGE

"We changed everything, including our name."

The meetings held early in the change process sent a very clear message: "If we don't fundamentally change this school, it might not be around in a year."

Similar to the leadership team at Manurewa, the Bayview leaders were not interested in being part of a school that was merely good; they were determined to have a great one.

In order to move away from the negative connotations of the past and forge a different future, after extensive consultation with their community and in a process largely led by students, what was once Rokeby High School relaunched with a new name, a new brand, and new uniform.

Similar to Cornish College, Bayview expanded to include grades 11 and 12. The school became part of an extended network of high schools and colleges called the Teggana Collective, a move that gave students more choice in which particular campus would best suit their needs during their final two years of learning. A level of excellence in learning became the expectation, and this was echoed with excellence on the sports fields with the launch of an elite sports "high performance centre," access to quality facilities through the sporting hub, and the forging of strong connections with a local football club.

Bayview's leadership team transformed the school's learning approach as well, deciding to focus on STEAM. Task forces of expert teams were built to address specific instructional problems, and these teams spent a year researching best practices, visiting schools nationally, and innovating how various approaches could be contextualized to their reality. Then they launched the ideas that made sense for Bayview. The key initiative that emerged from this process was a flexible learning program for the most disengaged students, which focused on personalized learning in unique classes built for them and located in a specific part of the school that they could be proud of. The next initiative, underway as we write this, connects to the growth mindset movement, and Bayview's leadership team is confident it will foster even more positive changes among staff and students.

WOORANNA PARK PRIMARY SCHOOL

"We set out to make our school as engaging as Disneyland."

When visitors come to Wooranna Park—and there are many who do—all of them comment on the space. And for a suburban public school, Wooranna Park's use of space is revolutionary and inspiring. Created by the students, with the assistance and guidance of an interior designer, the school is like no others that we have seen in our travels around the world. There are few walls, allowing learners to flow throughout the campus. The concepts of "classes" as isolated centers for year groupings doesn't exist; learning spaces are peppered throughout the campus, with some perfectly suited for group work and others designed for more quiet activity, tucked away in corners, on top of forts, or under bridges. Library shelves sit beside 25-foot-long spaceships. Art supplies are stored inside the roaring mouth of a dragon that is just able to squeeze its jagged tail under the ceiling. An amphitheater lies at the foot of a multilevel fort with a top floor that was too small for us to climb into but perfect for the three children we saw lying there, reading quietly. Straight edges are a rarity, noise is a near constant, and there is curiosity and amusement at every turn.

Wooranna Park's astounding use of space started small, with a redesign of the grades 5 and 6 classrooms into one big space that could accommodate more than 100 students, the introduction of team teaching, and the time machine that we wrote about earlier. But since then, the approaches have spread across the entire site. Wooranna Park seems like a playground, but stick around for a bit, and you'll see that the revolutionary space is matched by what's happening in regard to learning.

The key pillar of the school is not the space; it's student voice and self-directed learning. From grade 1, all students accept responsibility for their own learning even as they collaborate extensively, building understanding through interactions with their peers and the staff. Heavily influenced by the approaches of Reggio Emilia (10 staff members have spent significant time in Italy at Reggio Emilia sites), Wooranna Park has organized learning approaches to reflect confidence in students' capability and creativity. In practice, this means deep and authentic learning experiences created by students who set weekly goals with their teachers, plan the next stages of their projects, and negotiate work requirements. It means students shaping their own curriculum, engaging with areas of interest, and pursuing new skills and knowledge through investigation.

Workshops are also interspersed throughout the week to allow students to master the fundamentals necessary to complete the tasks they have set for themselves. All staff deeply value student opinion and, where possible, provide authentic forums for discussion, analysis, and reflection. In their senior years, students become actively involved in school parliament, providing guidance during cabinet member meetings with staff on contentious or pertinent issues. Four students are even official members of the teaching team and therefore able to engage in professional development to improve their skills.

Information and communication technology (ICT) is another area that Wooranna Park has invested in, with strong wi-fi, tablet devices throughout the school, and a blurry line between work done at home and during school hours. The Enigma Centre, which looks like something out of a *Star Trek* movie with its many screens, microphones, flashing lights, joysticks, and high-seated chairs, is one of the most impressive technology centers we have seen in our travels to hundreds of schools around the world. Remember, this a public school in one of Melbourne's more economically challenged suburbs. Students engage with complex video games, competing and collaborating with children on the other side of the planet. They also build their own blockchain currencies and track the wild fluctuations of the bitcoin donation that was gifted to the school (a situation that is proving to be very complex for central office bureaucrats to get their head around). When you walk into the Enigma Centre, it is unlikely that students will turn around to talk with you, so engaged are they in their learning, at a key moment in an online game, or in another world entirely, under their virtual reality headsets. The space is at the cutting edge now, but with inspired leadership coming from their head of IT, Kieran Nolan (an early mover and proud geek), they are likely to remain so for a good time to come.

And finally, there was the major change we mentioned earlier in this book. Acknowledging the need for distributed leadership, Wooranna Park's core leadership team decided to challenge every staff member to become a leader. It wasn't as simple as giving some people some new tasks and a new title; it was convincing all staff to step up all the time and lead on learning and building the skills necessary to do so. From an instructional leadership perspective, professional development sessions are held every fortnight, and they are almost always teacher led.

So is Wooranna Park as engaging as Disneyland?

It is pretty close, in our opinion. But just like Disneyland, behind the smiles and fun playgrounds there is something much deeper, more creative, and more intelligent going on. A peek behind the rides to glance at the machinery and complexity behind the scenes shows a labyrinth of learning and effort. We are inspired.

LESHER MIDDLE SCHOOL

"We created an elite learning experience that anyone can access."

Of all the schools we spent time in for this book, Lesher had the most powerful and conspicuous organizational culture. Students, staff, and parents had great clarity about what the school was and their role in it. And we've mentioned how the pride in the Lesher Vikings was on display everywhere. This work on culture was the biggest shift that the Lesher leadership team has made over the past decade.

Fifteen years ago, Lesher was a below-average middle school, surrounded by far more compelling options. The leadership team that turned things around was a highly competitive bunch, made up of elite sports coaches, National Guardsmen, and highly accomplished teachers. Quite simply, they expected everyone at Lesher would "work harder and care more" than the staffs at other schools. They expected Lesher staff to provide students with the kind of education they'd be thrilled to offer to their own children. And so the leadership team got to work building up and supporting their best teachers and openly recruiting for the kinds of educators willing to commit to working harder and caring more than most. In the words of Principal Tom Dodd, there was a concerted effort to "get the right people on the Viking ship, have them dig their oars deep to row, and for us all to move in the same direction."

Today's leadership team believes that happy teachers are better teachers, and they foster a culture of mastery, purpose, and autonomy, to reference the work of Daniel Pink (2009). They shelter the staff from "bureaucracy and nonsense" and openly encourage them to take risks with the goal of making things better for kids. There is an emphasis on instructional leadership, with 80 minutes of peer learning and collaborative planning every single day.

For us, Lesher's focus on culture is fascinating.

As we wrote this, we debated whether to direct so much attention to their "cultural shift" work, but the more we thought about it, the more right it felt. So many leadership teams that we work with see culture as just another component of what they do, part of "the tree of learning" that happens in a school; at Lesher, culture is the ground soil, the roots, and the trunk. For all that has grown from the school's push for excellence—and there are many accomplishments to tout, from first prizes at science competitions to sports trophies—it is the staff culture that underpins it all.

This is powerful.

Many schools today are turning to a data-driven focus on instructional leadership, but when they do not support it with powerfully positive cultures or strong transformational leaders, they rarely get the results they hope for. In the worst cases, too fierce a focus on instructional improvement results in high staff turnover, low morale, fear, and cautiousness— and we confess we saw evidence of this even at the excellent schools profiled in this book. Lesher proves the power of getting the culture right first and then pushing for the highest expectations on instruction and getting exciting results.

For example, Lesher's leadership team opened up the International Baccalaureate program, originally accessible only to the top 15 percent of students, to the entire student body. To use their own words, they "created an elite learning experience that wasn't elitist" but would instead provide world-class learning to all—from the children growing up in well-off families to children who are homeless and relying on food stamps.

It's easy to fall back on sports analogies when discussing Lesher, a place where school leaders sit in high-backed leathers chairs embossed with the Lesher Vikings insignia and conduct interviews with us on basketball courts emblazoned with the banners of sports achievements, so we will indulge in another one. Lesher is a school that was playing in an amateur basketball league before its leaders decided one day that it could win the NBA title. And the town of Fort Collins can be proud that their neighborhood school has essentially done just that.

CHICAGO TECH ACADEMY HIGH SCHOOL

"We showed that deep and powerful learning is possible for all children."

Whether it's referred to as project-based learning, inquiry-based learning, deeper learning, real-world skills, or something else, the learning styles espoused by schools like High Tech High (HTH) have generated a great deal of interest globally. As exciting as these approaches are, they still attract criticism related to effectiveness—particularly when the measurements are traditional signalers of success like effect sizes, destination data, and test scores. Additionally, there have been charges that while these approaches work well for children from engaged families and from wealthier demographics, they are not relevant for children living in situations of disadvantage. This assumption has been disproved by many schools, including a favorite of ours, the African School for Excellence in South Africa, the story of which we'll save for another book.

After signing a formal partnership with High Tech High and engaging extensively with influential HTH staff member Laura McBain, the ChiTech team got serious about developing project-based learning acumen. A group of education leaders flew from Chicago to San Diego for a weeklong intensive introduction to the approach. As Principal Linnea

Garrett told us, "You need to see it and live it for a couple of days to know it is possible."

Project-based learning is now the core learning approach at ChiTech. The halls are filled with student demonstrations. Classes are student led and multidisciplinary. The real-world applications of the learning provide realistic career pathways for students, and internships are offered from 9th grade onward, which is the same time that ChiTech's students begin receiving focused support toward college acceptance. A spot in a top university is a major goal at the school for a large number of these students from the South and West Sides of Chicago, many of whom will be the first in their families to pursue higher education. The walls and ceilings of the classrooms are covered with pennants and banners of colleges throughout the United States.

The other key shift made by the leadership team at ChiTech was to build teacher capacity. Those who had been working cautiously, perhaps focusing on meeting evaluation expectations, were encouraged to think bigger and put no limits on what was possible in their classrooms. They were empowered to try new things, learn quickly, and consistently share their learnings and improve their practice. As we discussed earlier, ChiTech's teachers began to meet for almost an hour every day, uniting a team that before had been lonely individuals working in silos. Annual whole-staff retreats were also launched, furthering the sense of unity and common purpose. All of these approaches have helped to build a team that is capable of meeting the biggest education challenges, and they do it every day.

JOHN POLANYI COLLEGIATE INSTITUTE

"We provided a wealth of opportunities for kids who, for too long, had gone without."

The leadership team at John Polanyi set a goal of providing world-class learning opportunities for young people who were not accustomed to accessing them. The most dramatic idea for transformation was to deliberately help all students build skills that will prepare them for future success. There was a particular focus on the skills of innovation and collaboration.

With the assistance of Manon Gardner, one of the Toronto School Board's senior superintendents, they forged a partnership with the Rotman School of Management at the University of Toronto to bring in the iThink program, developed by Professor Roger Martin. Initially integrated into a small business course for senior students, the program trained participants to solve real-world problems by considering contrasting analyses and feedback. It challenged them to come up with strategic solutions, rather than standalone ones. It was a hit. The students engaged with local challenges in partnership with a children's hospital and community charity, and the resulting levels of engagement and progress were so high that the school decided to extend the approach to the entire student body.

According to Principal Aiman Flahat, John Polanyi's whole-school approach to problem solving teaches students "how to think and be able to solve big problems while maintaining a vision, to be optimistic and not settle for quick fixes." Students have provided real-world and implementable advice to national parks, nonprofits, and even the school itself. And when asked to address the challenge "The school has already increased enrollment from 300 to 700; your challenge is to get us to 1,000 students," they had plenty of ideas to contribute.

If the John Polanyi leadership team were to sum up their approach to learning in one word, it would most certainly be *opportunity*, and we expect this is influenced to some extent by Aiman's own experiences as a migrant to Canada. "When students are given an opportunity to make a difference—when they have real problems to solve that are connected and related to community and organizations—it ignites a passion for them to engage in their learning," he told us. Students have traveled to Nicaragua to build schools. They have won innovation challenges and prizes across the world. And they are now the proud founders and managers of one of

Toronto's largest market gardens, which produces 7,000 kilos of fruit and vegetables each year.

But the leadership team wanted more. They also decided to transform the school into a center of excellence for STEM. Students can undertake specific courses in medicine, research, engineering, and business, and they engage in global STEM competitions using state-of-the-art technology. Those enrolled in these courses, some of them from the meanest streets in the city, graduate with work-ready certifications; others move on to college or university.

The leadership team's ambitious commitment to providing the best opportunities to the children of their community has become a reality.

After all our discussion in the previous steps of passion, listening, focusing, messaging, and culture, this step is actually the meat of the Change Leader Journey. It is what the Dream Teams actually did.

And when it comes down to it, getting your team to successfully navigate this step is the goal of the book. We want people like you to stand up together and lead change. After all, as Anne Frank said, "Ideas without action are worthless."

The next step is pretty darn important as well. It's where you scrutinize your initiatives to determine if the ideas you've implemented really were good ones. Specifically, you're looking to find out whether they made a difference for the children you are working so hard to serve.

9
PROOF

*How can we prove our change
initiatives have made the difference
we hoped they would?*

One of the reasons you're reading this book is to learn how innovative leaders change schools.

We've covered the work our Dream Team schools have done. We've shared how they innovated solutions to pressing problems, and how they made and sustained changes. But we have not yet discussed the critical question of whether all these changes really made a difference. There were certainly lots of outputs—activities conducted, programs launched, environments changed—but what were the outcomes?

In this chapter, we could have presented the results of in-depth academic studies conducted on each school we spent time in. We didn't do that. We could have presented page after page of tables with country-specific learning data. But we didn't do that. We could have taken sides on the many arguments currently under way about the proper use of data in education. We didn't do that, either.

What we have done instead is share the responses we received when we asked the Dream Teams a very simple question: *So, what changed?*

We listened for how they were using data, and we noted which data sets they pointed to when telling their school's story. We were interested in what they thought was important, what they had picked out of the often-complex business of running a school. We isolated the key trends we saw. Later, we'll propose how your leadership team may want to present the data shifts that you will achieve through your change initiatives.

here's what changed

LESHER MIDDLE SCHOOL

The key challenge the Lesher team wanted to solve was how to provide an elite learning experience for children in their community without being elitist. And if they wanted Lesher to stay alive, they needed it be more compelling as a school choice.

When we asked Waren Morrow—an assistant principal and the school's athletic and activities director—what had changed at Lesher, he answered immediately:

> *We are now one of the most impactful schools in our area. This has resulted in us being one of the most "choiced in" schools in the district, with more than 200 out-of-area applications each year and 100 already on our waiting list. While we perform above state levels on academic scores, we also do great on International Baccalaureate and excel in music and athletics. Our staff happiness surveys are extremely high, and we are known for our climate and culture. So basically, we have gone from a struggling school with declining enrollment to a thriving one.*

JOHN POLANYI COLLEGIATE INSTITUTE

The John Polanyi leadership team faced a challenge similar to Lesher's. Their school was uncompelling to the community and was not providing opportunities to its students. When we asked the "What changed?" question, many team members responded with stories of individual success and overall student progress. Principal Aiman Flahat said this:

> *It is the school of choice now, the "cool school" in the area.*
> *Parents are pulling their kids out of private schools and en-*
> *rolling them at John Polanyi. We were at 300 students a few*
> *years ago; now we have more than 1,000.*

MANUREWA INTERMEDIATE SCHOOL

The challenges at Manurewa were many, but boiled down, it would be fair to say that few were taking pride in the school and it was failing the community by providing a very poor learning experience.

When we asked the Manurewa leadership team "What changed?" they were the quickest of the Dream Team schools to point to numbers, and they had them on the tips of their tongues. They were ready to share all kinds of documented changes and eager to acknowledge how these had helped them engage partners and foster momentum. We learned that

- At the start of the transformation period, Manurewa was the most frequently vandalized school in New Zealand; over the past nine years, they were able to reduce their annual vandalism repair budget from $120,000 to just $4,222.
- Since 2008, student attendance has risen from 80 percent to 93 percent.
- Academic progress is tracking up. Here's a sample of their latest numbers:
  —In reading, only 29 percent of the grade 7 intake arrive at the school performing above the state average; by the end of grade 8, 60 percent of the student body test above the stage average.
  —In writing, only 23 percent of the grade 7 intake arrive at the school performing above the state average; by the end of grade 8, 60 percent of the student body test above the stage average.

—In mathematics, only 29 percent of the grade 7 intake arrive at the school performing above the state average; by the end of grade 8, 54 percent of the student body test above the state average.

- The school now must enforce the district enrollment zone after becoming oversubscribed by the wider community; in other words, parents who were supposed to send their children to a different school, per district guidelines, want to send them to Manurewa.

CORNISH COLLEGE

At the beginning of the Cornish story, the existing school model was set to be shut down, unable to operate financially with an enrollment of only 300 students. At the school's fifth birthday celebration in 2017, leaders proudly announced an enrollment of 701—a 250 percent increase.

CHALLIS COMMUNITY PRIMARY SCHOOL

The key challenge that the Challis leadership team faced was that children were arriving to the primary school already well below state levels. Critically, after a year of learning, these children had made little improvement.

Remember, a lot of changes at Challis focused on investing in the community's children long before they reached school age. In response to our question, the leadership team pointed to a formal study conducted by a local university and said proudly,

> *We have smashed it out of the ballpark with our data before the children reach us. [Our community's children] were below state average for literacy and reading and not making any improvement. The data now show [they] start at about the West Australian state average.*

A few years into the innovations, Challis has seen a 40 percent reduction in the prevalence of vulnerability for children entering preprimary education. Particularly significant has been the improvement in the language and cognition domain. At the start of the change effort, 25 percent of the children scored in the lowest percentile; the current data show that figure has dropped to 10 percent. The report found that up to 95 percent of the children who have been through the Challis early intervention program are outperforming those children who have no exposure to the program. Quite simply, they are seeing that their approach works.

BAYVIEW SECONDARY COLLEGE

The leadership team at Bayview set out to change because their school was uncompelling and had a terrible community perception . . . and because they were warned by system leaders that they had to turn the school around before the risk of being closed became real.

When we asked, "What changed?" the team was quick to point to several key data sets:

- Increased enrollment overall, up by 50 percent over the last two years alone
- Successful additions of grades 11 and 12; the 80 students enrolled for 2018 represent a 300 percent increase from the first year of the initiative
- Grade 7 enrollment at the highest it's been in 15 years
- A dramatic reduction in suspensions, down from 135 to 40 over a single school year
- Significant improvement in staff culture such that the school now has educators and students eager to join the learning community

JEREMIAH E. BURKE HIGH SCHOOL

The Burke was a school that was officially failing—placed into turnaround status and the leadership team given a clear directive to improve or be replaced. Here are the data sets the Burke's leadership team pointed to when we asked them what had changed:

- Over eight years, the graduation rate increased from 32 percent to 74 percent.

- During the same period, the attendance rate increased from 82 percent to 92 percent.
- The number of students performing above state averages for mathematics rose from 28 percent to 67 percent in the first five years. By 2017, 90 percent of students had demonstrated proficiency gap narrowing—an exceptional result.
- Over five years, the number of students performing above state averages for English/language arts jumped 29 percent to 70 percent.
- The number of suspensions dropped from 525 in 2009 to just 16 in 2014.
- Fifty percent of the Burke's current graduating class plan to pursue four-year college degrees.

And a final historical note: Jeremiah E. Burke High School was the first school in the state of Massachusetts to exit turnaround. It took them three years.

WOORANNA PARK PRIMARY SCHOOL

One of the oft-repeated mantras at Wooranna Park is "Change the system, not the child." In a school that knows how radical it is, leaders are not afraid to prioritize more unorthodox data over traditional measurements. Overall, the school performs just below the state average, which is not unforgivable, seeing as it's situated in one of the state's most economically challenged suburbs. Wooranna Park's public response to these results is summed up in this statement:

> These measurable outcomes need to be considered along with our philosophical belief that there are many other important outcomes of our behaviors that are indicative of a student's progress and overall development. Creativity, resilience, disposition to learning, self-motivation, and an ability to collaborate are highly valued at Wooranna Park and difficult to measure on a numeric scale. Records of these types of behaviors are

maintained and monitored in a variety of ways including observations, digital recordings, tracking sheets, student self-assessments, portfolios, conferencing, and reflections.

Principal Ray Trotter is also quick to mention the Singaporean child from a very prosperous background who has moved to Melbourne specifically to engage with the learning approaches at Wooranna Park and the student team who progressed to the European robotics championships in the global Lego League.

CHICAGO TECH ACADEMY HIGH SCHOOL

At the beginning of the current leadership team's tenure, ChiTech was operating well short of its potential. The school had great promise it was not delivering. The new leaders' goal was to provide a high-quality learning environment for very disadvantaged young people, and things have begun to track upward, with the increases jumping exponentially each year. When we asked, "What changed?" these are the facts the ChiTech team pointed to:

- The graduation rate has risen from 55 percent to 77 percent.
- The "freshman on track rate," used to predict high school graduation rates and target students for intervention, has risen from 63 percent to 93 percent.
- The annual dropout rate has fallen from 5.7 percent to 1.8 percent.
- The percentage of current students who have amassed college credit has risen from 22 percent to 42 percent.
- Sixty-three percent of senior students plan to enroll in college next year.
- On the Illinois Department of Education's "5 Essentials Survey on School Climate and Culture," the ChiTech teachers' rating of "collaborative teachers" has risen from 51 to 77 (the district average is 67); their rating of "trust" has risen from 57 to 82 (the district average is 67); and their rating of "collective responsibility" has jumped from 38 to 62 (the district average is 69).

JOHN A. LESLIE PUBLIC SCHOOL

The leadership team at John A. Leslie focused exclusively on changing their instructional approaches during their first year, then pivoted to an engagement strategy based on student voice and entrepreneurship. Here are some of the results they achieved over a five-year period:

- In reading, the number of students performing at year level rose from 58 percent to 85 percent.
- In writing, the number of students performing at year level rose from 53 percent to 90 percent.
- In mathematics, the number of students performing at year level remained steady at 56 percent; this was a standout result in a province where math scores dropped 11 percent overall.

The John A. Leslie team clarified that their results were even more remarkable considering the external challenges affecting their students' academic success. The Toronto District School Board uses a metric called the Learning Opportunity Index (LOI) to quantify the disadvantage levels of the children and families served by each school in the district. Schools are then ranked in the region based on their LOI score, with the most disadvantaged school receiving the rank of 1. Over the five-year period of the change initiative, John A. Leslie's ranking score moved from 211th most disadvantaged to 126th, meaning that they were improving their students' learning even as the community they drew from became poorer.

measuring the right things in your school

Leadership teams driving successful transformation have clear processes not only for deciding which traditional data metrics they will shift but also for designing and measuring new metrics where there are no system metrics that will provide the proof they need. Here are some things to think about as you build up your own data sets.

KEEP AN EYE ON TRADITIONAL METRICS

Education systems across the world are increasingly data driven, enabled by all kinds of policies and initiatives that collect data across many different aspects of education. Your team will no doubt be familiar with standardized testing to measure learning and growth (often with a dominant focus on measuring literacy and numeracy), regular reports based on teacher judgment and tests, demographic data, attendance and engagement data, student behavior data, student and parent perception data, and more recently, harder-to-measure points such as well-being and emotional intelligence. These data often form the basis of school reviews by district superintendents. They are what the media use to compare schools in jurisdictions, and they are often what parents focus on when considering where to enroll their child.

No doubt you are also aware of school-level challenges to the weight placed on these data sets, especially standardized testing results. But the reality is that as much as some of us push back on traditional measures of success as unfair or limited, for now they don't look like budging. This means you need to determine how to best use traditional data sets to guide and document the change you are creating.

The schools that have the most success using these kinds of data as "proof points" are those that analyze results at the individual, class, school, district, and national levels. They don't just look at the final numbers; they interrogate the data, both to help them determine their focus (earlier in the journey) and to prove how the change they have created affects outcomes at the different levels. When a superintendent or director shows a leadership team summative data, that team should be able to break them down and indicate a narrative of growth across various aspects of the school.

So while the traditional, system-mandated data measures are often narrow, they are still important and useful. All of the Dream Team schools had traditional system measures as part of their proof of change and impact. They pursued changes in these data sets, and when they were unable to shift the results, they explored why and questioned what they needed to do differently. In your school, clarify which traditional, existing system metrics you will use to validate and inform your change efforts, and make sure you are tracking these. If nothing else, these data sets will confirm your ongoing alignment with district-, state-, and national-level metrics and help you find support to drive the change you are trying to achieve.

COPY THE INNOVATORS

If you want to be a Dream Team, tracking traditional metrics is not enough. Because children are so fascinating and complex, they deserve our best efforts to measure and improve a much wider range of outcomes.

The good news is that there are organizations, researchers, schools, and individuals constantly designing new ways to measure and prove the impact of educational innovation. Where you can, you should copy what they do! Search for the teachers, schools, and systems that are successfully changing the areas you are focusing on, reach out to them, and see how you might learn from or adapt their approaches. Talk to other leadership teams from schools within and outside your network and absorb the most relevant approaches into your school. You don't need to create more work for yourself. Chances are, the brilliant ways to measure and collect the proof you are looking for are already out there. Find them. Use them.

CREATE YOUR OWN METRICS

If you have looked far and wide and haven't been able to find great ways to prove your impact, then you will need to create ways of your own. Remember that every type of measurement approach was created by someone—a real human being who brushed their teeth and put on their jeans one leg at a time (if they were jeans-wearers). So why not your human beings, your people, your team?

Oftentimes, what you'll be looking to capture will be qualitative data, such as how staff, students, or parents are perceiving the school. These often take time and resources to collect effectively and can be the complex longitudinal narratives that emerge over time. If you are struggling to come up with ideas about how to do this, lean on your newly acquired ideation tools (see Chapter 7) and pose a "how can we" question to get your team generating ways to capture proof of the achievements you value the most.

Oh, and when you do nail a new and innovative way to measure something and create compelling proof, share it widely. So many educators are stuck, forced to pursue outcomes that are already being measured, even as we know these are not always the right things to pursue or even value.

measuring what you value

A major takeaway is that the majority of the Dream Team schools were armed with compelling traditional data sets that they were proud of and were able to present clearly. Yet many of them were quick to follow up these data sets with measurements that they found more exciting and more meaningful.

Greg McLeod at John A. Leslie shared this:

> *What the traditional measurements do not show is the increase in student engagement. Students felt they could approach me or staff with ideas at any time. They ran professional development sessions on coding for staff. The environment of the school changed with students engaged in deeper learning and far more meaningful and powerful technology use. Generally there was a feeling that the school was a special place, and there was such a feeling of pride.*

The Wooranna Park team, as we highlighted earlier, remain frustrated by traditional data sets. Principal Ray Trotter stressed,

> *Not all the "big data" is important. Big data rules us, and the small data that comes from the teachers is never put up against the big data.*

Wooranna Park's decision to step back from a focus on more traditional data sets has not come without consequences. Some educators in the region see it as the school's Achilles' heel. Wooranna Park has struggled to consistently produce strong outcomes on traditional data sets, largely due to leadership's decision to strive for more radical types of learning and less mainstream metrics. Other Dream Teams we spent time with have capitulated to a greater degree, reconciling their passionate beliefs on how children can best learn and be assessed with finding the wins that they need to satisfy the system leaders. And truthfully, it is hard to deny that anecdotally Wooranna Park is doing incredible things with engagement, particularly when they recount stories like a parent saying, "My son has been waiting for years to come to this school and learn in the giant dragon."

Whether the members of Wooranna Park's leadership team stay the radicals they are today or give in to the more traditional demands of their system remains to be seen. If they can create powerful new measurements, the hard times will surely be worth it. As Anna Bligh (2015), the former premier of Queensland in Australia once said, "Don't look at my bruises; look at the hole in the wall, and then go through it yourself."

As an example of a new kind of proof of an initiative's success, consider the drop in vandalism rates at Manurewa. One of the school's leaders told us, "We were the most vandalized school in the country, but that changed completely. Our skate park has never been graffitied since it was built, and last year we only spent $4,000 on school damage, down from $120,000."

Consider that Lesher was initially worried about the rising rates of students and families aligning with the "Opt Out" movement—declining to sit for the standardized achievement tests that purport to measure student, teacher, and school success and even the standardized aptitude tests (like the SAT) that have traditionally served as a gateway to higher education in the United States. The leadership team has come to applaud these decisions and is seeking new ways to measure and document learning. One possible way forward is articulated by the Mastery Transcript Consortium (2018), which asserts that "while the high school transcript aims to assess student progress and performance, it is a broken instrument that no longer serves students, teachers, or the world outside our school walls." The group is working to grow an alliance of independent schools and create a new transcript that allows students to gain micro-credits for skills including analytical and creative thinking, leadership and teamwork, and global perspective.

At ChiTech, while they are working hard to improve traditional data sets and succeeding, they also draw upon the power of the demonstration model so common in project-based learning. Exhibition nights are a major deal for the school, bringing in hundreds of members of the community and acting as a significant motivator for students during the semester.

Interestingly, though, ChiTech's leadership team was very careful with the data sets that they shared in the early years of the transformation. Their goal was to inspire their teachers to think big and try new things, and they believed that if they were looking over their shoulders all of the time and thinking about data, this wouldn't be possible. As Assistant Principal Tiara Wheatley told us,

> In the early years, we didn't make a lot of noise about data, simply because it wasn't great and it was demoralizing. Now, as things have improved, we track and share data all the time. We seek out the numbers to fine-tune what isn't working and keep asking ourselves whether our expectations are high enough.

Almost all of the Dream Teams had at least one person who absolutely loved working with data—and it was rarely the principal. Lesher's Tom Dodd was candid on this point:

> A parent cares about climate, culture, and compassion, so this is what I focus on and share with them. I am weak on data— maybe it is my biggest flaw—but I have great leaders who are brilliant in that area, so we work as a team.

At Challis, Lee Musumeci had a similar response:

There is a love for data at this school, but I am not the number-cruncher. Our deputies built data trackers and follow outcomes very closely.

It is worth noting that these two principals who owned up to not being particularly focused on traditional numbers themselves were both named as their respective countries' national principal of the year.

The most effective schools and districts we spent time with were passionately working to assess changes in creative and compelling ways. In Ontario, they are grappling with how to measure a change in someone's impression of themselves, where they feel they have more value, voice, and power. In Victoria, Australia Education Changemakers has been working on how to measure the engagement of a student through a project titled The Passion Index. There is much to be done in this area, and it remains an avenue of inquiry worthy of more effort.

Finally, all of the leadership teams knew that to move students, parents, the community, system leaders, donors, and partners, they had to move people's hearts. The most effective teams could do both, sharing funny, inspiring, or touching anecdotes of change, and then catalyzing the power of this through clear and credible data.

As a leadership team, how are you walking the fine line between reporting on traditional data sets to keep some stakeholders happy and leaning into more creative but no less important data sets that truly help you to demonstrate the change you are making? These are courageous decisions to be making as a team, and the work requires you to believe in yourselves and keep at the front of your mind the reasons why you are leading this change in the first place: *to make things better for kids.*

You've done great things as a leadership team, and the positive outcomes of your change efforts are becoming clear to all. But every journey has a final step, and it's not always an easy one to take. That's what we'll look at next.

10
THE FUTURE

How can we make the change last... and what's next?

Staying Power
Aaron Tait
Dar es Salaam, Tanzania, 2008

We had been at the school for a year, but it was time to go.

The stamp in our passports said it all: "Thirty days—no further extensions."

Kaitlin and I had been trying for 10 months to get a work permit legally, but every application had been knocked back. So we decided to return to Kenya, accepting an invitation to help grow the capacity of a village orphanage and education project. As we packed our bags on our final night at the school, we knew there was much to celebrate.

The school looked fantastic. It had been fixed up, landscaped and painted by the kids, staff, and members of the community. A global bank had come on as a donor, and the library and lab were now filled with great books and science equipment that students were using enthusiastically. Daily attendance had risen from 30 percent of enrolled students to 90 percent, and the staff had grown from a low of just three teachers to eight brilliant educators who came to work every day, passionate about helping the kids. Our school farms were growing crops that were being consumed in students' daily meals, and the students were running a wide range of businesses, earmarking a percentage of profits to support school operations and putting the remainder in savings for higher education. The goal we had set on our first night had been to pass 10 kids through the national exams; we had passed 14, and some of them were enrolled in architecture and law at a local university.

The year had been huge, and we were exhausted—gaunt from multiple bouts of malaria and dysentery. But we were happy to be alive, having had a few close scrapes.

There was not much to pack that night. Our plan was to travel light back to Kenya, and we'd given away much of what we owned to students and community members. For some reason, our old T-shirts had been the most popular items—the height of fashion for the local kids.

The value of those shirts was underscored a little later that evening, when a student called Thea came to say goodbye. Kaitlin had invited her over for a cup of tea and a small gift (the two of them had been close). When Kaitlin held out a necklace inscribed with the word *rafiki*, Swahili for "friend," Thea examined it, looked up at Kaitlin and then over her shoulder at me. "Sister Kait," she said, "the necklace is nice, but do you have any T-shirts left?"

Kaitlin had no more T-shirts, but they kept chatting, sharing tea, and then Thea headed back to her dormitory. A few minutes later, Kaitlin asked me a simple question: "Are we nothing more than a T-shirt to these kids? After everything we have done—including almost dying a few times, have we made a difference here? Was it worth it?"

I didn't have an answer, but I was saved by another knock at the door. It was Jon—an amazing kid from a very poor family. He had worked hard all year and had passed his exams. But that night I was tired, and the question from Kaitlin had thrown me. On answering the door, I held my hand up, shook my head, and said, "Sorry, Jon. No more T-shirts, my friend."

Jon held up *his* hand to interrupt me. "I didn't come for a T-shirt, Mr. Aaron," he said. "I came to say thank you to you and Sister Kait for changing my life." And then he walked away into the darkness.

I closed the door quietly and turned around to look at Kaitlin. She was smiling.

"It was worth it," she said.

real change lasts

It has been more than a decade since that day. Today, Jon is an agricultural scientist, and he and Aaron are still friends on Facebook.

The sad part of the story is that for all of the success of the year, Aaron and Kaitlin are the first to admit that they failed to build sustainability into the school they had led in Tanzania. Forced by an immigration department deadline to leave on short notice, they hadn't had time to train new leaders to take over. They know they did what they could during that one year . . . and also that they did nothing after they left, a pair of 25-year-olds with only a few hundred dollars between them.

Aaron and Kaitlin drew on this very tough apprenticeship in East Africa—the many mistakes they made and the lessons they learned—when they built their nonprofit organization dedicated to changing the lives of people in poverty by finding brilliant local entrepreneurs, helping them scale their work, and supporting that work for the long run. We also brought these learnings into our work at Education Changemakers.

Spending time with this book's Dream Teams, it became clear to us that while some make great strides in a few years, it often takes five to seven years to achieve real and effective change in a school. In fact, some of the most important years for a leadership team are the final few, where they bake in the changes and make them sustainable. Based on what we have experienced over our decades of combined work in education and social change, with a measure of humility for the mistakes we have made, and drawing on the wisdom of the Dream Teams, here is how we think your team can increase its chances of making your changes sticky and sustainable.

FOSTER TALENT

Beyond the learning and engagement results that we documented from the Dream Team schools, one realization jumped out very powerfully.

The most effective leadership teams were effectively "principal academies."

Immersed in an environment with exceptionally impressive examples of instructional and transformational leadership, educators naturally became equipped with the skills, confidence, and desire to become leaders themselves. At John Polanyi Collegiate Institute, for example, across the six years of change Aiman Flahat led as principal, eight educators on his team were invited to lead other schools as principals. At John A. Leslie Public School, eight leaders were promoted to principal positions during Greg McLeod's seven years in charge. Over five years at Manurewa Intermediate School, seven of the deputies moved on to be principals at other schools. And if you look at Principal Iain Taylor's entire career to date, 17 of his deputies have become principals themselves.

These promotions are obviously bittersweet. The schools lose key leaders from their leadership teams, and it can be difficult to train others to fill the gaps they left behind. But for the system it is a win. As a leadership team, ask yourselves if you have created the kind of learning and capacity-building culture (from both an instructional and a transformational approach) that makes your school a "principal academy."

This book is about teams, and as much as possible, we have focused on how leadership *teams* have created change. Yes, all of the principals of the schools we spent time with have won multiple awards, and some of them have even enjoyed a certain degree of fame in education circles. Under such circumstances, there is the possibility that a cult of personality will develop, where the staff and community (and sometimes the leader too) believe that if the leader were to leave, things would collapse. We even heard this at one of the Dream Team schools, when a teacher confided that if the principal left, "the school would fall apart." Another principal expressed this fear openly: "There is a real danger that someone could come in with a different belief structure." This is a real concern.

Conversely, there were a number of Dream Team schools where the principals were confident that their leadership succession is secure. At Jeremiah E. Burke High School, Principal Lindsa McIntyre didn't even hesitate when asked if there were leaders who could take over: "You could flip a coin between most of the leaders and one of them would do an amazing job." At Manurewa, Iain Taylor was equally emphatic that there were leaders on staff who could step up into the principal job. In fact, he had already been testing this after effectively handing over the school to his associate principal for all of 2016 while serving as the president of the New Zealand Principals Foundation. At Lesher Middle School, Tom Dodd felt both of his deputies could step up to lead the school—and that their hunger to do so was clear and inspiring. When Gill Berriman of Bayview Secondary College took leave while her partner was recovering from heart surgery, she let her assistant principal lead the school for three months and was thrilled with how he performed. At Chicago Tech Academy High School, Principal Linnea Garrett could easily name three leaders she felt were capable of moving into her role and leading the school in the positive direction in which it was headed.

RECRUIT PEOPLE INTO THE CULTURE

Eager to see "the Challis way" continued and built upon in the school, Challis's leadership team is careful about who they hire. Generally, they offer permanent positions to the most passionate and mission-aligned graduate teachers who join straight from their practical university placements. As we mentioned earlier, for 17 of Challis's "18 leaders," being a part of this team constituted their first formal education leadership position. At John A. Leslie, at the beginning of the transformation period, there were only three novice teachers (teachers in their first five years in the profession) on staff; that number had more than doubled by the end. Hiring people who fit the culture and who can be brought into the way things are done at a school through a powerful induction has proven to be an effective way of baking in changes and fostering sustainability.

As a team, think about whether the people you are bringing in to your school and the way in which you are bringing them are helping to strengthen the strategy and the culture, or slowly erode them.

DON'T REST ON YOUR LAURELS

Manurewa is a school that has totally changed over the past nine years. But they are not lazy in their success. "Change is constant," Principal Iain Taylor told us. "We are always getting better."

This ongoing commitment was evident in all the Dream Teams. At Lesher, they "tweak the focus area each year by listening to people and continually clarifying the mission." At the Burke, they start the year by looking at the data and figuring out where they need to go next: "Less is more with our priorities, which are likely to align with our focuses on equity and the whole child." Each year, all of Lesher's professional development and most of the class observations focus on the new goals they set.

At Bayview, working groups spend an entire year focusing on the next learning priority for the school, and powered by research and insight, they launch it the next year.

As a practical tool for leadership teams, some of the most powerful improvements each year were strategized at whole-staff retreats that leadership creatively found funding for. In fact, for the two schools in the most disadvantaged and challenging contexts (ChiTech and the Burke), the staff retreats were seen as vital. The time away, spent in community with one another over good food and in honest conversation, brought the team together and prepared them for the big year ahead.

CELEBRATE SUCCESS

The highest-functioning teams that we spent time with made the celebration of success a major priority. At Lesher, every meeting starts with 15 minutes of celebration when people shout-out other staff members for the good things they've done.

At Manurewa, there is a weekly staff awards ceremony where "Vernon's Visionary" is announced (the winner gets to house "Vernon," a soft toy turtle, on their desk for the week), as is "Carer of the Week" (who has custody of a big back scratcher for seven days). Staff at the school also receive handwritten postcards from leaders and even the occasional motivational text messages late on a Friday night. As Iain says, "Success breeds success, so we find it and share it."

At the Burke, successes are celebrated with community barbecues (heavy on the Caribbean food), and a local band plays before the big announcements.

At Challis, the leaders try to understand how different staff members like to be thanked and celebrate them in that manner.

How are you celebrating your successes, or how else might you? And remember, celebrations don't always have to be public or come from the principal. Indeed, ChiTech's Linnea Garrett believes the best way to uphold the culture of celebration is to make it the work of the entire leadership team rather than something that's wholly on the principal's shoulders.

ENGAGE WITH AWARDS PROGRAMS

Many of the Dream Team schools have won major awards in recent years for their work.

Manurewa was named as the most engaging school in New Zealand at the 2017 Prime Minister's Education Excellence awards, before going on to win the prize of the best school in the country.

The Burke won the prestigious "School on the Move" prize from Edvestors in Boston.

Aiman Flahat and Greg McLeod were both named as "Outstanding Canadian Principals," and at John Polanyi, two teachers (Vernon Kee and Rahim Essabhai) each won the highly selective Prime Minister's Award for Teaching Excellence.

Tom Dodd at Lesher and Lee Musumeci at Challis Community School each won National Principal of the Year from their respective countries' peak leadership body.

The majority of the Dream Team schools began to actively engage in major awards programs in the latter years of the school transformation, applying for consideration or being nominated by those who saw the good work going on. Now these schools' trophy cabinets are full—and psychologically, these awards have meant a lot to the school communities.

The credibility and publicity that comes with awards make them a strategy your leadership team should certainly consider as you look to make noise about your work. Have you been holding back from applying to these programs? Perhaps it is time to step up and ensure that people know about the great work that is happening!

ENGAGE WITH THE MEDIA

All the Dream Teams used media channels to make positive noise about their school. Some were more deliberate with about this than others. For example:

- The John Polanyi leadership team was active across TV, radio, and newspapers, and the Manurewa leadership team joked that they had the media department on speed dial to spread positive messages through the community.
- The ChiTech team worked hard to push back against negative coverage of the South and West Sides of Chicago by sharing stories of student success with local channels.

- At Bayview, the team found Facebook to be the most powerful way to engage with their community. They used their page to share success, mobilize people for events, and respond to questions.
- At John A. Leslie, Twitter and the school blog were the most commonly used methods to share the school's approaches with other educators in Toronto and around the world.

There are certainly differing scales with which schools engage with media, ranging from those at one extreme who remain quiet and hope the media stays away, to others who only return e-mails from the communications department at the head office, and then to those who are media darlings. If your leadership team wants to engage with the media and your community, here are a few guidelines.

Be aware of your key message and communication objectives.

Before you begin engaging with the media, determine what your key message is. In a sense, this is also your brand—who you are and how you want to be perceived by the public. As a leadership team, determine whether you are safe and traditional, or edgy and disruptive. Are you looking to change a mindset? Do you want business and government leaders to take notice of you?

Also think about whom you want to excite. If you want parents and their children engaging with your school, make that clear in your messaging. When you are being interviewed on the radio, on TV, or for the newspapers, stick religiously to your soundbites and messages to increase the likelihood that what you say will make the evening news or the front page. For example, at ChiTech, the leadership team was eager to share the success of the school with the public and help dispel the notion that schools on the West Side were failing young people. Their brand was that students coming to ChiTech were accessing a world-class and future-focused learning experience.

Make nice . . .

Journalists need to file stories regularly and fill newspapers (or websites).

So give them stories.

Start by keeping an eye on your favorite newspapers, websites, blogs, magazines, radio stations, and TV shows. Start reaching out to them (even sending e-mails directly to specific journalists whom you like). As often as you can, serve up great content, sending press releases accompanied by high-quality photos and inviting media representatives to events. If you do this, before long, they will start reaching out to you to see if you have anything happening that they can write about. And the best part is, rather than paying for media exposure, you'll be getting it for free! Manurewa's local newspapers loved the school and were constantly sharing news of awards that the students and staff had won. The newspaper staff were also a regular presence at the school's cultural community days.

As a leadership team, consider setting a target to reach out to at least one media agency each month.

. . . But know that the media are not always your friends.

Unfortunately, bad news sells more than good news. This means that while many journalists will play nice with you for a period, they may also choose to paint the school, or your district, in a very bad light. So remember that everything is usually on the record with the media and that if they smell smoke, they will look for fire.

The key is to stick to your key messages, keep the relationship professional, and don't reveal to your media contacts or put them in a position to overhear anything that you aren't willing to have on the front page of the newspaper. Perhaps the most famous former teacher to have made this mistake with the media is Gordon Brown, the former prime minister of England. After a campaign event, he drove off with his press microphone still on, so everyone could hear him call a voter he had just been speaking with "a bigoted woman." Brown lost the election.

Social media can be more powerful than traditional media.

As we're writing this, the current platform of choice for educators is Twitter. For parents, it is Facebook, and for students—well, that is very difficult to keep up with! Social media channels change in popularity, so your leadership team should be responsive to what avenues are the best to engage with. The trouble is that many schools get this wrong.

A great metaphor for social media is that it is like a big cocktail party. Imagine walking into the party to find thousands of people in the room, all chatting while a band is playing loud jazz music. You try to stand on a chair, yell your 280-character announcement to the room, and then head home. Chances are this approach is not going to be all that fruitful. Yet this is how many people treat their social media channels, yelling a line occasionally and wondering why they don't get more likes.

In the social media cocktail party, you need to get in that crowd and mingle. Have conversations. Connect. Find out what other people are interested in, and then tailor your conversations to suit that. In other words, build a following by engaging with people, responding to them, and serving up content that they will be attracted to. On Twitter, feel free to tweet away as much as you like. On Facebook, there are two rules of thumb: thou shalt not post more than three times a week, and thou shalt make those posts a blend of something interesting for your community (a relevant news article, something about the school) and questions and actions that prompt engagement or response. With Instagram, it is all about high-quality images and telling the stories behind them. With YouTube, you want to keep your videos under three minutes.

At John A. Leslie, the leadership team used Twitter daily to profile great learning that they could capture around the school. It became such a great motivator for the staff that they would often send a text message to a leader that they should pop into their classrooms because a great learning moment was happening at that instant!

Branding will benefit you.

Right now, there are hundreds of thousands of advertising teams thinking up ways to convince us to eat more, buy more, exercise more, sleep more, do everything just a little more so that we will be . . . happier, maybe?

If you can't beat them, join them. See if your leadership team can't put forward a school brand that is more compelling and life changing than a pair of shoes or a cheeseburger.

Manurewa, for example, has four school houses (their whanaus) that the students are nominated into. On their first day at the school, they are given a rubber bracelet with the colors and mottos of their house. Wearing a whanau bracelet is not compulsory, but as we walked around the school, we saw one on nearly every teacher and student. Kids wear their bracelets to the skate park after school, to sports practice, to the shops, and in front of their siblings, who one day hope for a bracelet themselves. Manurewa has literally turned their students and staff into walking billboards, constantly exuding a positive and united message about their school.

Is your school inspiring a loyalty as strong as this for the changes that you want to see in your community? If it's not, what can you do to change that?

OPEN YOUR DOORS

Opening your doors so people can visit the school not only shares your great ideas with more educators but also raises the pride of your team and turns them from participants in the change to models of it.

Of the 10 schools we spent time in, Wooranna Park was one of the most visited. We saw all kinds of people walking through the site—and those were only a fraction of the visitors who come every year. Initially, they marvel at the creative physical spaces, and then the staff step in to encourage them to take a closer look at the learning approaches (which are far more important). Wooranna Park receives many e-mails monthly, and staff struggle to answer even a fraction of them.

Challis holds open houses a few times a year. On each of these days, there are 100 visitor slots. Most times, all the slots are filled.

John A. Leslie Public School had visitors from across the world come to the school in the period of the school transformation, and constantly brought visitors from other schools and government through to see the learning environment. Not bad for a little primary school in the suburbs of Toronto.

STAY ALIVE

If there was one thing that all of the leadership teams didn't have sorted out, it was work-life balance.

They were all obsessed with improving their schools and making things better for kids and totally overworked themselves, some flirting dangerously close to burnout.

We are not really sure what to make of this.

On the one side, perhaps you need to be crazy to work as hard as these teams and in order to truly change a school? Perhaps we need leadership teams who are willing to give it their all and sacrifice a whole bunch to make things happen?

But also maybe as a profession, and as the members of leadership teams, we need to be nicer to ourselves. Because the truth is, we need all of the Dream Team leaders to be doing what they're doing. And we need you to do the same.

Find encouragement when and where you can. At the Burke, Lindsa McIntyre joined a professional community of her peers that gave her space to vent and receive support. ChiTech's Linnea Garrett found the same approach helpful to her. Greg McLeod at John A. Leslie gained energy from walking the halls and talking to kids.

The old saying "the shoemaker's son has no shoes" is so true for educators. We spend so much time working for other people's kids that we sometimes neglect our own or ourselves. As we get closer to the end of this book and the Change Leader Journey, see if your team can't take a moment out to check in with how you are doing and what you might need to keep doing it.

scaling what you've created

There is no doubt that the Dream Teams profiled in this book created some great things. They were so great that we couldn't help but wonder if more students in more places should be able to enjoy them. So at every school, we asked, "If your idea worked for 100 students, could it work for 1,000?"

The leaders would usually nod, confident that they could reach kids across their school, or perhaps at nearby schools. Then we would ask if it could work for 100,000 students. Or a million. Or a billion. Alas, when we started throwing around these big numbers, we seemed to lose all of them. And the fact is, beyond offering the occasional school visit to other educators in the region, none of the leadership teams had actively been able to—or had even thought seriously about—scaling their ideas beyond their sites. All of them thought that their solution was so contextualized that it couldn't be replicated as well somewhere else.

As impact entrepreneurs, we always think at big scale, asking ourselves how an idea can have as wide a reach as possible. With our own work at Education Changemakers, the ideas that we created in schools are now accessed in face-to-face workshops by tens of thousands of teachers a year, and many more find these ideas online. As we mentioned earlier, the nonprofit that Aaron and Kaitlin started now supports and invests in hundreds of entrepreneurs across Asia and Africa, changing hundreds of thousands—and one day, millions—of lives. When we accelerate startups through our various programs around the world, we challenge the entrepreneurs we work with to build business ideas that will change at least a million lives. To get into the Singularity University in Silicon Valley, you need to be working on an idea that has the potential to impact one billion people. This is big thinking, and a pretty interesting way to approach the world.

In education, though, we are not so good at scaling ideas.

Richard Elmore at the Harvard Graduate School of Education has been lamenting this for decades. In a 1996 article called "Getting to Scale with Good Educational Practice," he explores the question of how good education practices can move beyond pockets of excellence to reach a greater proportion of students and educators (Elmore, 1996). The premise of the piece is "Why has replicating great work and programs on larger scale been such a difficult and vexing issue?" Why, indeed? Elmore's article is now decades old, and although we now have ideas about the why, we don't have a definitive solution to the how.

We wrote this book to identify the key steps that occur when a brilliant leadership team comes together to change their school. And while we had hoped to uncover some gems of advice from our Dream Teams about how they were scaling their ideas, we didn't. It was perhaps the only disappointment of this project for us amid its overwhelming positives. They haven't cracked the "difficult and vexing question" yet, and neither have we.

But it is better to light a candle than to curse the darkness, so here is what *we think* school leadership teams should be thinking about as they work to scale their ideas.

REMEMBER THAT IT TAKES A SPECIAL KIND OF PERSON

In their brilliant book *Scaling Up Excellence,* Stanford academics Robert Sutton and Huggy Rao (2014) talk irreverently of the kinds of people who work toward large-scale ideas: "What drove them crazy, kept them up at night, and devoured their workdays was the difficulty of spreading excellence to more people, and more places" (p. 1). We work with many people like this, and we are probably these kinds of people ourselves, but one character that sticks out for us is Noni Masina, the cofounder of the African School for Excellence in South Africa, a brilliantly affordable and high-quality school for some of the country's most disadvantaged children. When we met Noni, she told us her goal immediately—a world-class education for every child in Africa. Her story is a powerful one: as the only student to graduate from university in her township, she was determined to change her community and, one day, her continent. Not all of us have stories like Noni or visions this big, and the reality is that maybe we don't all need to think like this. As Bobby Kennedy said in a 1966 speech at the University of Cape Town,

> *Few will have the greatness to bend history itself, but each of us can work to change a small portion of events, and in the total of all those acts will be written the history of this genera-tion. It is from numberless diverse acts of courage and belief that human history is shaped.*

We love this quote, and we see the truth of it when we see great leadership teams changing schools. But a little part of us still feels that maybe, just maybe, one of these teams—maybe even yours—will create something powerful enough to bend history.

TURN THE IDEA INTO A SOCIAL MOVEMENT

History has shown us repeatedly that the largest changes to societies and systems come from social movements. Be it civil rights over the last century, gender equality over the last few decades. or marriage equality more recently, dramatic shifts have taken place when large numbers of people stand up behind an idea. These ideas are often countercultural, with the original drivers of the movement facing ridicule, opposition, or even criminal ramifications for their efforts.

Santiago Rincón-Gallardo from the University of Toronto has worked closely with both Richard Elmore and Michael Fullan to delve into how education innovations can be scaled as social movements. He points in particular to the Learning Community Project in Mexico, which was able to take a small tutoring concept created by a nonprofit and scale it to more than 9,000 schools in a short period. Rincón-Gallardo and Elmore (2012) believe that "social movements act as forces for social innovation because they operate in fundamentally different ways from public agencies and work against certain fundamental patterns of culture and practice in mainstream, established organizations" (p. 477).

What are the chances that your idea can be scaled in this countercultural manner? Rather than growing its reach through the system, can you grow it outside, or in spite of, the system?

An example of this in practice is the TeachMeet movement, which began in Scotland as a teacher-led idea that would move away from an increasingly corporate professional development sector. Our good friend Ewan McIntosh gave the informal gatherings the name "TeachMeet," and the idea scaled across the world.

Victor Hugo wrote, "There is one thing stronger than all of the armies of the world combined, and that is an idea whose time has come." If your team's innovation is truly "an idea whose time has come," do you have the courage to take on the system and bring your innovation to scale as a social movement?

GET POLITICAL

As the saying goes, there are many ways to skin a cat, and so too are there many ways to scale an idea. Indeed, while the Learning Community Project was working to scale like a social movement, they also had one of their key leaders (Dalila López) invited to join the Department of Innovation at the Mexican Ministry of Basic Education. In this role, López was able to evangelize the model to other senior players in the Ministry and help to positively influence the government's decision to scale the tutoring approach to more than 9,000 schools. So as teachers grew the innovation in their own time and in their own classrooms as part of a social movement they identified strongly with, the Learning Community Project was able to legitimize the idea through a large-scale program backed by the government.

If this is an avenue that excites your team, you need to determine who your Dalila López is. Who is the individual who will make a concerted effort to move into a key role at the highest levels to effect systemwide change?

Similarly, system leaders should also be looking at high-potential innovations that have been created in schools by teachers or leadership teams, and they should have the courage to provide the resources and time for those teams to scale the concepts widely. In Toronto, for example, after finishing up their tenures as principal, both Aiman Flahat and Greg McLeod were invited by the system to share their approaches with schools across the region. Similarly, a number of leaders at Jeremiah E. Burke believed that they had powerful ideas to share with underperforming schools in Massachusetts. They envisioned themselves as a sort of task force, and they were eager for the system to deploy them in this role.

MAKE IT SIMPLE

We have worked with several schools that have come up with breakthrough ideas but have really struggled to share these with others. When we asked one of the Dream Team schools about whether they had shared their ideas widely, their response was telling: "Very few people would be able to understand what we do."

So the key is to make what you do understandable. If we think of concepts that have scaled to the point where large numbers of people have heard them and loosely understand them, we can point to "Stop, drop, and roll" in the event of a fire and the uniquely Australian approach to reducing skin cancer, "Slip, slop, slap." (That's slip on a shirt, slop on some sunscreen, and slap on a hat.) These simply stated ideas, coined by someone at some time in history, have likely saved many, many lives.

We often train teachers in our innovation program to think of their innovation as a recipe that they can teach others how to implement in their own schools. Can your leadership team dramatically simplify your approaches to a format that others can understand, learn from, and maybe even apply themselves?

BUILD YOUR IDEA WITH SCALE IN MIND

When you begin to think about scaling your idea, recognize that there is a big difference between building something that will reach tens of schools and something that will reach thousands. If you are thinking of going really big with your idea, it can be helpful to think of the idea as a body-builder. Yes, the first thing people will notice are the obvious attributes—huge biceps and quadriceps, for example—but what's powering these huge bodies and allowing them to function are the underlying organs pumping blood and oxygen. To scale an innovation, you need to make sure there are systems in place to keep it running.

An example of an education idea that has been built with scale in mind is Bridge International Academies, a controversial but no doubt fascinating school network that started in Kenya and now has hundreds of schools reaching more than 100,000 children. In the network's first year, it announced a strategic plan to open 3,000 schools and was able to attract investment from people like Bill Gates and Mark Zuckerberg.

While scaling innovative school models has seen rapid growth in Africa, in the United States, it's not been so easy. In a 2015 piece published on *Slate*'s blog Schooled, Jessica Huseman identified a number of charter school networks that scaled ambitiously only to have to dramatically back away from these ambitions. Edison Schools, for example, partnered with 130 schools at its height; at the time of Huseman's writing, that number had dropped to 5. In 2000, Advantage Schools, another charter chain, enrolled more than 10,000 children across the country. By late 2015, it enrolled zero.

So, in short, going "large scale" is exciting, but failure is a very real possibility. As they say in the world of entrepreneurship (and gambling), big risks, big rewards.

LAUNCH A NEW SCHOOL OR SCHOOL MODEL

In almost every program we run, there's one line we inevitably hear. So enthused by the ideas that they are creating, and so inspired by the brilliant educators that they are working with, someone exclaims, "We should all start a school together!" This is a very tempting idea for some leadership teams, and we have seen this eventuate in a number of ways.

The most obvious (and controversial) of these is to start a charter school. While the overall results of charter schools in the United States are not as strong as many would like, there are certainly strong pockets of success. KIPP Academies, for example, educates tens of thousands of children at hundreds of schools across more than 20 states. According to a 2015 report, they are able to report a 93 percent graduation rate, with 83 percent of their students moving into college (Tuttle et al., 2015). Indeed, in 2010, the U.S. Department of Education awarded the KIPP Foundation a $50 million Investing in Innovation (i3) scale-up grant, which the company used to foster a leadership pipeline and more than double the number of students served, from 27,000 to nearly 60,000.

Yet charter schools are not the only avenue that leadership teams can take if they want to formally launch a new school or network of schools based on their ideas. Queensland educator Cally Nielsen, an alumna of one our programs, created a new approach to learning for disengaged students at her school, Bundaberg State High. Following strong results in her initiative's first year, she approached local government and gained approval to take over an abandoned site and launch a new school. In Victoria, Brett Pedlow did the same thing, building out an idea through a yearlong program of ours before he went on to launch La Trobe Valley FLO (Flexible Learning Option) to great success.

Launching a new school as a leadership team is not as farfetched as it might sound. Maybe it's in your future.

FOSTER A PIPELINE OF HIGHLY EFFECTIVE TEACHERS

As we all know, the most important factor in the success of a child in school is teachers who support his or her learning. Equally, successfully scaling an education innovation is largely dependent on the quality of the people who are part of this new learning approach. The unifying feature among all the Dream Teams that we spent time with was that they had exceptional individuals with passion, intelligence, and a commitment to improving the education of the children in their school. So, although it seems awfully simple, ideas can scale across regions or beyond when there is a pipeline of brilliant leaders being trained to move into new positions of authority. The most effective new school networks promote the majority of their staff internally rather than relying on new recruits. Some of them, such as San Diego's High Tech High, run their own in-house training academy.

As we have mentioned already, a number of the schools that we spent time with functioned almost as "principal academies," demonstrating a proven track record of building up the capacity of junior leaders and then wishing them well as they moved on to their own schools. At Manurewa, there was such a strong desire to foster leaders for the education sector that Principal Iain Taylor began floating an idea with the system that would see him with a half-time load as principal of the school and the remainder of his time spent facilitating a principal training academy that would embed high-potential leaders into the school for three months to understudy the Manurewa team.

Is this something you may want to consider at your school? It takes confidence to believe that your school is so strong that others can learn from it, but if more high-impact schools leaned into this work, the results could be very powerful for our systems.

BALANCE MORE AUTONOMY WITH GREATER ACCOUNTABILITY

Something interesting happened as the Dream Teams became more effective and produced stronger results over the course of their change processes. Often, the more they improved, the less autonomy they had.

We can point to the Burke as a strong example of this—a school that had great freedoms that the leadership team leveraged in the early years of the turnaround process. But as the Burke moved out of official turnaround status, the team found many of these freedoms taken away. While we don't believe that pure autonomy to the point of anarchy is the way forward for education, we do feel that when system leaders increase the levels of autonomy afforded a strong leadership team while also increasing accountability, the results will more often than not be positive. There is more research to be done in this area, but it remains a debate in which system leaders should eagerly engage.

SCALE IN A WAY THAT WORKS FOR YOU

In sectors beyond education, there are some creative approaches to scale we might learn from.

Scale like a hippie.

In this mindset, everything is cool, and you are trying to spread your ideas around the world just like the hippies wanted to spread peace and love. When you share an idea openly (and often, for free), you let go of the need to tightly control what happens with it. TeachMeet is a great example of this. Teachers share their ideas, expect no financial reward, and allow people to use the new approaches as they please. Practically, scaling like a hippie could mean creating a PDF toolkit that you share widely, maintaining a blog that documents what you are doing, or presenting often at events and at other schools to share your idea.

Scale like McDonald's.

This is the franchise model. If you visit a McDonald's in Boston, Beijing, or Berlin, you'll see that much of it is familiar. They are cooking the cheeseburgers a certain way, the Happy Meal toy that month is probably something from the latest Disney movie, and the golden arches are emblazoned everywhere. If you open a McDonald's franchise, you pay for the right to do this, buy your produce from the McDonald's supply chains, and don't stray from the rules that are set.

In an education sense, this is what Bridge Academies have done. Many of the schools teach the same curriculum; in fact, it's likely that many of the schools will be teaching exactly the same curriculum at exactly the same time. This model allows your team to keep control of your approach, but you lose the freedom of your local operators to contextualize the ideas in ways that they deem necessary.

Scale like an Irish pub.

Let's say that after your McDonald's dinner in Boston, Beijing, or Berlin, you feel like having a pint of Guinness. If you find the nearby Irish pub, there will likely be wooden floors, some black-and-white photos on the wall, and if you really want to fit the cliché, some dusty typewriters and vintage knickknacks around the place. And of course your Guinness will be there waiting for you. Yet no one has made the owner of the Irish pub sign anything to say that she will create her bar in a certain way. There is no rule book she is abiding by. Instead, she intrinsically understands what an Irish pub usually looks like because she has seen some before, so she works roughly within these guidelines.

In education, an example of this is schools that are applying design thinking skills in their school. There is no central body telling them what they must or must not do; instead, they pick up ideas from other schools and educators who are following this approach and work to embed them in a way where classes feel connected to the idea of design thinking but still locally relevant.

Scale like a Silicon Valley tech company.

Once an idea has been proven in Silicon Valley, the most high-potential companies engage with venture capitalists and raise huge war chests, up to hundreds of millions of dollars. With this kind of money, you can invest in great people, incredible facilities, and the things that you are going to need when you hit your expected levels of scale.

In education, we saw this approach with AltSchool, a Silicon Valley education venture that raised $175 million from investors with the goal of building a network of system-changing schools. Going this big means that success, if it comes, is on a large scale, and that failure can be equally as dramatic. The AltSchool story is still being told, but leadership teams with large ambitions would do well to look deeper into the AltSchool story to give them some insights before they follow this approach.

Scale with others.

And the last way to scale that we want to touch on happens to be our favorite. It is when you scale your ideas with someone else. In business this means joint ventures, mergers, and acquisitions, and these tools can be used in education as well. In fact, we have a saying that we repeat frequently: "It is amazing what can be achieved when you don't care who gets the credit." Aaron merged his entrepreneur acceleration nonprofit with another similar organization, and within two years, the result was a five-fold increase in funding and a 15-fold increase in impact. At Education Changemakers, we have collaborated with some of the world's largest technology and training companies to drive far greater impact than we could have achieved alone.

So there you have it—some things to think about if your leadership team wants to go big and scale the ideas you have created to impact many more children. Swinging big is not for the fainthearted, but it is a thrilling way to work, and the rewards, if they come, can be massive. Did you know that while Babe Ruth had the highest home run average, he also led the league in strikeouts? What kind of hitter are you? Someone who plays it safe and tries to get walked, or Babe Ruth?

when the chapter is ending

Most of the teams profiled for this book worked together as a close unit for five years in order to achieve the success they sought.

When we spent time with them, all of them looked back with fondness on what they had achieved, particularly those leaders who had already moved on. Some even evoke a sense of nostalgia for the present—a feeling that they are in the middle of something great and a fear they may never again in their career experience these same feelings of purpose.

Ultimately, schools are only as good as the leaders and teachers in them and the students engaging in the learning. Now, and certainly for the foreseeable future, these schools are very good indeed. But people move on, times change, and chapters come to an end.

As a leadership team, one of the most courageous things you can do is to recognize and act upon the realization that perhaps it is time to move on, hopefully to even greater heights. Here is what we learned from the schools about what you can do as a team as the change effort comes to an end.

ACHIEVE ONE LAST GOAL

In 1951, Joe DiMaggio shocked America by announcing his retirement from the New York Yankees and from the game of baseball. A few months earlier, he had helped the Yankees to another World Series title, their ninth in his 13 seasons with the team. DiMaggio was a three-time MVP and had made the All-Star team every year he was with the Yankees. He set a record for home runs in a rookie season with 29, a record that stood until 2017. DiMaggio's most stunning achievement in baseball, however, was the hitting streak he put together during the 1941 season, where he got a hit in 56 consecutive games. It's a record that is still standing—an achievement referred to by a Harvard statistician as "the most extraordinary thing that ever happened in American sports." Yet at the height of his fame, Joltin' Joe walked away.

As leadership teams, we can set similar standards of excellence and also have the courage to call it a day at our height.

One of the most powerful ways to do this is to set bold targets and work as a united leadership team to hit them. At Challis Community Primary School, the team does not talk about moving on until they hit a number of key goals they have set for themselves. At the top of that list is closing the gap between Aboriginal and non-Aboriginal children in Armadale. The Bayview team declared that they won't stop until they get the school enrollment to 350 students. At Wooranna Park, Principal Ray Trotter wants to see his last project, The STEAM Centre, fully operational before he moves on—in his case to retirement and reflection on his stunning contributions as an educator.

Does your team have an ambitious goal that you want to hit? Do you have the courage to move on once it's achieved?

MAKE WAY FOR THE NEXT GENERATION

As should be clear now, a common by-product of the change led by the brilliant leadership teams we spent time with is a new bunch of high-capacity leaders. As we saw, some of these leaders move on to serve as principals of other schools, while others have such a deep love and commitment to their school that they stay, hoping to keep contributing and perhaps one day assume the principalship. At Lesher and the Burke, for example, it was clear there were leaders who were ready to stand up and take the reins of the school as principals. Making way for their passion and intelligence is one of the noblest and bravest things a senior leader can do.

Some leaders also acknowledge that their skill set may have been just the thing for one challenge but is not quite the thing for the next. The company Google seeks outs this type of leadership—characterized by individuals with both the chutzpah to lean in and solve a problem and the humility to lean back and let someone else lead when the situation changes. This certainly happened at Cornish College, where once the parents had saved the school, they very clearly handed leadership over to the educators who would take it forward.

As an individual veteran leader on your team, consider: is it time you stepped aside, or do you still have work to do?

CONSIDER TAKING YOUR IDEAS TO A DIFFERENT NEXT LEVEL

Leading a school as a principal, assistant/deputy principal, or department head is an incredible honor, and it's one that none of the people we spent time with took lightly. However, many of them saw their role in a school transformation coming to an end after a period of five to seven years, by which time they had set their sights on roles in education that could see them achieve impact at larger scale.

Many of the leaders we spent time with believed that they could achieve powerful things as a district superintendent or in another key position of authority; as we wrote this book, Greg McLeod and Aiman Flahat were just that in Toronto. There is a confidence that comes with achieving powerful changes in a school, and our systems need practitioners like them—ones with scars and insight earned on the battlefield—planning the next moves.

On the other hand, maybe you'd like to make a lateral move and try your hand in a different school with a different team?

Lots of the Dream Team leaders found this idea appealing. They wanted to stay in a school and keep working with kids. At ChiTech, Linnea Garrett acknowledged that the leadership team had more work to do, but she also was excited by the idea of one day trying to transform another school on the South or West Side of Chicago as dramatically as they had transformed ChiTech.

BUT BEFORE ANYTHING, TAKE A MOMENT TO BE PROUD OF WHAT YOU HAVE DONE

As leadership teams, we don't often have a chance to stop for a moment and reflect on what has been achieved.

At Cornish College, one of the parents on the leadership team stated with clear emotion, "We had a real impact on people's lives. I don't think I will ever do something as powerful as this again." Another parent said, "This is a highlight of my life. Every time I drive down that school driveway I am so proud."

All of the teams who were still in the midst of the change knew they were part of something special. Those who had moved on missed these times—the heady mix of purpose and risk and the inspiring thought that every day, they were changing the lives of the children in their care.

CONCLUSION

Moving On
Dave Faulkner
Halls Creek, Western Australia, 2009

I reversed slowly out of the driveway, careful not to wake the neighbors.

The girls were already asleep in the back of the car. They had become comfortable with long drives and were likely to breeze through the 10 hours that were ahead of us.

We had a deadline.

I was starting on Monday as the district superintendent for the Barkly District, one of Australia's most challenging territories and, by size, perhaps the largest education region in the world.

The leadership team at Halls Creek had achieved a lot in three years.

My personal goal and greatest passion had always been to provide an education that I would be happy for my own kids to receive. I had demonstrated this commitment by enrolling our two daughters in a school that had been labeled "the worst school in the country."

In the early days, we had listened—to everyone. We sat for hours under trees listening to community elders talk about the type of school they wanted for Halls Creek. We sweated in the sun, playing basketball on the heat-cracked basketball courts, hoping for a chat with the kids at the end of the game over Icy Poles (that's an Australian ice pop) so we could get a sense of how they saw their school.

We'd kept listening every step of the way, building and revising based on what we were hearing. We hadn't always gotten it right, but by and large, the community had been on board. In the week before my family and I left, amongst the swimming races and barbecues at school, the quiet thank-yous and handshakes and knowing nods from them had meant a lot—little glimmers of honest gratitude from a famously shy people.

Almost every teacher in the school had led a project. In all, they got 37 up and running—everything from horseback riding to art, technology to business skills. Once they truly knew that every idea they brought us would be heard, and once they realized that we kept saying yes to everything they asked for, their creativity had been astounding. And they had made the radical timetable change we proposed a reality. The total shake-up of our distributed leadership structure—bringing local staff into the mix, many of them without education backgrounds—had been smooth because of our teachers' appetite to try new things. The grim and stressed-out staff I had first met were now smiling, benefiting almost as much from our new well-being programs as the kids were.

The team had done an amazing thing in Halls Creek.

Together, we had raised attendance from 37 percent to almost 80 percent. We had risen to the top of the rankings of all schools in our socioeconomic category in reading, writing, and mathematics. Ours was certainly no longer the worst school in the country. We had so many parents engaged in the school, and our cultural campouts were always fully attended. Excellence was also happening on the sports fields, with newly earned regional and national trophies in basketball and horseback riding, and a football program that was so successful that one of our students would one day go on to be an early-round draft pick into the national league. The school had won awards, been profiled nationally, and received its fair share of visiting government leaders, academics, and philanthropists, all eager to figure out what we had done.

I thought it was pretty simple. We had built a capable team who gave everything they had to provide a great learning environment for young people.

My deputy principal would be taking over from me. Honestly, though, I could have flipped a coin between my deputies; either of them would have been perfect for the job. For his part, he was thrilled to be the new principal, even though he was sad to see our Dream Team broken up.

But it was time for me to move on. I was barely 30, but I was ready to see if I could be part of leading a team across an entire region. And my goal was clear. I would start in the Barkly District, but the world was a big place, and I wanted to be part of building the capacity of as many leaders as I could so that they could assemble their own Dream Teams and lead change in their schools. In this way, I'd be doing my bit to make things better for as many kids as I could in my lifetime.

I put my foot down on the accelerator and headed for the highway.

best of effort

So that's the end of the Change Leader Journey and of this book. But it is certainly not the end for you! When you put this book down, your attention will no doubt be back on your school and the life-changing work that you do there every day. We've moved through a lot together, but remember that it can all be summed up by the simple 10-step Change Leader Journey, which charts the work to be done.

You start by aligning your passions as a team for the change journey ahead with great honesty.

Then maybe you eat a slice of humble pie as you commit to truly listening to your staff, students, parents, and community leaders and gain a better idea of where you should be taking the school.

With bold clarity, you set your three focus areas for change.

With a mix of respect and bravado, you demand autonomy from your system leaders, while also ensuring you can provide the wins that they need to see.

You truly move people and engage your community powerfully with your ideas.

You spread responsibility across the school and generate energy by having *more* leaders in the school rather than fewer.

You inspire an awesome culture of innovation across the school to help you come up with the solutions you need to change things, and then you make these solutions a reality.

Armed with the right types of data, you prove that the ideas work.

Then you summon the courage to go together (by bringing more people in), go big (by scaling), or go somewhere else (by deciding to move on).

Some of you may be at the start of the journey right now, excited to get moving and changing things. Some of you have realized during this book that you are halfway through a journey, and with some tweaks you can increase your chances of it having a good ending. Some of you are coming to the end of a journey and starting to think about the next one, the next chance to change a school and make things better for kids.

Remember, wherever you are in whatever journey you're on, you won't get everything right. Sometimes you will get tired. Sometimes you will upset students, their parents, their teachers, or your leaders. Sometimes the data won't come back quite as positive as you had hoped. Sometimes your best people will leave. Sometimes, and most tragically, a student will slip through the cracks. But at the end of the day, it is all worth it, and if as a team you work as hard as you can, success will come in many forms.

As the great Dream Team player Michael Jordan said,

> *I've missed more than 9,000 shots in my career. I've lost almost 300 games. Twenty-six times I've been trusted to take the game-winning shot and missed. I've failed over and over and over again in my life. And that is why I succeed.*

On your journey, we wish you the diligence of the Bayview team, the culture of the Lesher team, the local insights of the Burke team, the entrepreneurship of the John A. Leslie team, the commitment of the John Polanyi team, the creativity of the Wooranna team, the parents of the Cornish team, the distributed leadership of the Challis team, the success of the Manurewa team, and the raw courage of the ChiTech team.

We would also wish you luck, but as we have seen, Dream Teams make their own luck. So instead, we will wish you the best of effort.

You've got this.

—Aaron and Dave

REFERENCES

Bergmann, S., & Brough, J. A. (2007). *Lead me, I dare you! Managing resistance to school change.* Larchmont, NY: Eye on Education.

Bligh, A. (2015). *Through the wall: Reflections on leadership, love, and survival.* Melbourne: HarperCollins Australia.

Elmore, R. (1996, Spring). Getting to scale with good educational practice. *Harvard Education Review, 66*(1). Retrieved from http://www.project2061.org/publications/designs/online/pdfs/reprints/5_elmor1.pdf

Fabry, M. (2015, November 27). How the Slinky sprang into stores 70 years ago. *Time.* Retrieved from http://time.com/4127170/slinky-70-years/

Fullan, M., & Quinn, J. (2015). C*oherence: The right drivers in action for schools, districts, and systems.* Thousand Oaks, CA: Corwin; and Toronto: Ontario Principals' Council.

Hattie, J. (2009). *Visible learning: A synthesis of over 800 meta-analyses related to achievement.* New York: Routledge.

Heath, C., & Heath, D. (2010). *Switch: How to change things when change is hard.* New York: Crown Business.

Huseman, J. (2015, December 17). These charter schools tried to turn public education into big business. They failed [Blog post]. Retrieved from http://www.slate.com/blogs/schooled/2015/12/17/for_profit_charter_schools_are_failing_and_fading_here_s_why.html

Kawasaki, G. (2005, December 30). The 10/20/30 rule of PowerPoint [Blog post]. Retrieved from https://guykawasaki.com/the_102030_rule

Kennedy, R. F. (1966, June 6). Day of affirmation [Speech]. Delivered at the University of Cape Town, South Africa. Retrieved from http://rfksafilm.org/html/speeches/unicape.php

Kotter, J. P., & Cohen, D. S. (2012). *The heart of change: Real-life stories of how people change their organizations.* Watertown, MA: Harvard Business Review Press.

Mastery Transcript Consortium. (2018). Homepage [Website]. Retrieved from http://mastery.org/

Miralles, F., & Garcia, H. (2016). *Ikigai: The Japanese secret to a long and happy life.* New York: Harper Collins.

Naik, G. (2006, November 14). A hospital races to learn lessons of Ferrari pit stop. *Wall Street Journal.* Retrieved from https://www.wsj.com/articles/SB116346916169622261

Pink, D. (2009). *Drive: The surprising truth about what motivates us.* New York: Riverhead Books.

Rincón-Gallardo, S., & Elmore, R. (2012, December). Transforming teaching and learning through social movement in Mexican public middle schools. *Harvard Education Review, 82*(4), 471–490.

Robinson, V. (2007). The impact of leadership on student outcomes: Making sense of the evidence. Retrieved from http://research.acer.edu.au/research_conference_2007/5

Steinberg, A. (1997). *Real learning, real work: School-to-work as a model of high school reform.* New York: Routledge.

Sutton, R., I., & Rao, H. (2014). *Scaling up excellence: Getting to more without settling for less.* New York: Crown Business.

Tait, A., & Faulkner, D. (2016). *Edupreneur: Unleashing teacher led innovation in schools.* Milton, QLD: Wiley Australia.

Tuttle, C., et al. (2015, September 17). *Understanding the effect of KIPP as it scales: Volume I, Impacts on achievement and other outcomes.* Final report of KIPP's Investing in Innovation grant evaluation. Mathematica Policy Research. Retrieved from http://www.kipp.org/wp-content/uploads/2016/09/kipp_scale-up_vol1-1.pdf

Vallerand, R. (2010). On passion for life activities: The dualistic model of passion. *Advances in Experimental Social Psychology, 4,* 97–193.

Woo, E. (2015, April 1). Gary Dahl dies at 78; creator of Pet Rock, 1970s pop cultural icon. *Los Angeles Times.* Retrieved from http://www.latimes.com/local/obituaries/la-me-gary-ross-dahl-20150401-story.html

INDEX

The letter *f* following a page number denotes a figure.

ABOUT THE AUTHORS

 **Aaron Tait** is the cofounder of Education Change-makers (EC) and its director of innovation. A global leader in innovation for impact, he is at the forefront of a movement of "entrepreneurs changing lives." Aaron is the lead author of the 2016 book *Edupreneur* and the leader of the EC Labs education accelerator, and he works to integrate entrepreneurial approaches into EC's work with educators. He has built his outside-the-box thinking over a diverse career that has seen him complete seven years of active service as a decorated military officer, lead a secondary school for street children in Tanzania and an orphanage in Kenya, complete three master's degrees, and graduate from Cambridge University. Aaron is a cofounder of YGAP, an international development not-for-profit, and the creator of the organization's impact model, which has supported hundreds of impact entrepreneurs across three continents and changed the lives of hundreds of thousands of people living in poverty. Aaron advises companies and governments across the globe on impact entrepreneurship, is a Village Capital fellow, and in 2015, was named by the Foundation for Young Australians (FYA) as the Australian social entrepreneur of the year. You can reach Aaron at aaron@educationchangemakers.com or follow Education Changemakers on Twitter @educhange.

Dave Faulkner is the CEO and cofounder of Education Changemakers and has emerged as a global leader in education innovation. An in-demand chair and keynote speaker for some of the world's largest education events, Dave has shared the stage with education innovators including Ken Robinson, Angela Lee Duckworth, Anthony Salcito, Sugata Mitra, and former Australian prime minister Julia Gillard. Dave's education leadership journey began as a principal of an Australian school when he was only 24, for which he was awarded Young Australian of the Year (Western Australia) and Young Leader of the Year (Western Australia). He undertook a succession of school and regional improvements as a principal and regional director, matching grassroots understanding with system-level insights and bringing a relentless focus on ensuring all students can access a great education. Dave is a global leader in education startups acceleration, works with thousands of educators each year, and advises senior government, education leaders, company executives, and leading philanthropists across the globe. You can reach Dave at dave@education changemakers.com and on Twitter @d_faulk.